To the memory of my beloved mother, Alberta Dabney-Burrell, and as a gift to all those students who have sat in my classes and have been my constant inspiration, I dedicate this story of my life with its "feet of clay" and "pinnacles of glory" balanced by the hand of the Master Teacher.

Acknowledgement

To Dr. Elaine Giddings, who encouraged me by reading and critiqueing a part of this manuscript.

To my daughters, Mildred, Katie, Julie, and Katrina, and to my granddaughter, Carla, who gave me the courage to write certain chapters.

To God, who gave me this life and my limited skills, taught me how to use them, and guided me with a loving hand, I am thankful.

Contents

Rebellion

I trudged wearily up the littered steps of the subway kiosk and emerged into the heat-deadened New York street. Even the minute excuse of a neighborhood park wore a hang-dog appearance in mid-July, mirroring my own feelings of dejection. Three hours earlier I had quit my job. Now miserable, heartsick, frightened, I wondered where to turn.

Never before had I walked out on a position. I'd always prided myself on being a steady, dependable employee, but this time I had no other choice. I could no longer stand my employer's insulting ways. Due to her nagging, demeaning manner I'd lost twenty pounds, and my nerves were taut as harp strings.

America was just recovering from the depression of the 1930s, and for the second time in a year I found myself unemployed.

"Why, God—why has this happened to me?" I breathed as I walked down the busy street. "Do I really deserve this?"

I'd done well at my former position as city clerk. In four years I'd received four promotions.

But then that job became a civil service appointment, and I lost out. But I had soon found employment as receptionist in Mme. Wolter's Studio of Speech, Voice, Diction, and Drama. I'd been elated—such an excellent learning opportunity. I had *learned* all right! Learned how to run a business, how to meet and satisfy people, and how *not* to treat employees!

Upon reaching my boardinghouse I dragged myself up the steps and down the long, narrow hall to the high-ceilinged room I called home. La Chat, my Maltese cat, diverted my attention with his usual scolding for my all-day absence. In piteous cat language he insisted he was starving, so I fed him. Then I went downstairs to the basement kitchen I shared with other boarders. Its bleak dampness further depressed me. The food I prepared held no interest. I only picked at it; then left, carrying my troubles back upstairs with me.

"Why, God?" I began all over again. "Why am I having such a hard time? I don't hurt anyone. I'm a good Christian—I think. I go to church, pay tithe when I'm working, and remember the Sabbath day. God, You've promised to care for me. Must You push me to the wall?"

Momentarily, I lifted my eyes to the small shaft of light sifting through my only window. "I know about prayer, God," I continued. " 'Pray without ceasing,' and 'Take your burdens to the Lord and leave them there.' " Bitterly, I flung out the words, "All right, God. Here's a burden for You. Show me how to get another job!"

Sinking down on the bare floor beside my bed, I let my pent-up tears flow. But I kept talking, "God, You know I need work. I hate charity, but I have no idea where to look for work—"

As clearly as if He were talking to me on my telephone God's answer came. "You can teach church school."

"Church school again?" I gasped. "No, Lord. No." I thought of the children I had loved; but visions of dissatisfied parents crowded in, and I recoiled from the idea. "Please, God, not church school!"

Silent tears flowed once more. But finally, gulping down a sob, I challenged, "Lord, I won't spend one penny for a postcard to *ask* for work in one of Your schools. But if "— I weighed it long and hesitantly—"if You call me, I will go."

Relief swept over me. No one would call me to teach church school this late in the summer; all teachers had been hired. I undressed and tumbled into bed. I was quite sure God couldn't use a rebel like me, but I was wrong about God.

Answer from Heaven

Three days had passed since my daring challenge to God. The next day the postman stopped at my door and called, "Special delivery for Miss N. Burrell."

Could this be the answer?

"James L. Morgan, President, Oakwood College," I read in the upper left-hand corner of the envelope. How in the world did he locate me? James and I had been classmates at South Lancaster Academy in Massachusetts over ten years earlier. Since that time we had met once or twice at a camp meeting. We'd only exchanged news of friends and classmates. Now, why was he writing to me, and how did he know where to find me?

I ripped open the letter, and my eye flitted down the page: "The faculty of Oakwood College has voted to invite you to join our staff . . . two positions are open . . . teaching in the Education Department or Dean of Women."

Tears rushed to my eyes. God had not forsaken His rebellious child. Thrilled, yet also apprehensive—I had never taught in college before—I dropped to my knees beside the bed. "Thank You, Lord. I'm sorry I doubted Your promise to care for me. If this is the kind of church school You want me to teach, yes, I'll go. And I think I'll try deaning, for a change!"

On the first Thursday in October 1939, I boarded a train at Penn Station to begin my journey south. La Chat rode in a cage beside me. I settled comfortably into an upholstered seat in one of the coaches and wondered with some foreboding what God had in store for me.

I'd grown up in the North, and the stories I'd heard of lynchings and other atrocities against my people had seemed terrible, yet far away and no threat to me. How would I fare in the deep South? I breathed a prayer to God and felt my apprehension lessen as words of an old spiritual came to mind: "Lord, don't move that mountain: Give me strength to climb over it." After all, God had given me the call; I must trust Him for the outcome. I settled back in my plush seat and read my Bible as the train passed through familiar territory.

In Washington, D.C., where I had to change trains, I received a foretaste of "southern hospitality." Along with other passengers of my color, I found myself ushered into a coach just behind the baggage car. None of my fellow passengers seemed surprised, so I tried to sleep as the train chugged on through the night, reaching Chattanooga, Tennessee, in the early dawn.

After a long, tiresome wait in Chattanooga, the next train we were to take puffed in. This time the "colored" were assigned to the back half of an old, dirty coach. It angered me a little, but I endured it.

Hours passed. Winding its way slowly through cotton patch after tobacco field and on through waving stalks of corn, the train pulled up at every gathering of two to five houses. There were always post office signs with names like Fernville or Hollywood or some other misnomer underneath. Where was Huntsville, Alabama? The college was located there, and I had thought from the map it couldn't be far from Chattanooga. The sun grew hotter and hotter, and I grew hungrier and thirstier mile by mile. When I thought I could stand no more, the conductor called out "Huntsville!"

What a relief to step off that train. A neatly dressed, pleasant-faced man stepped forward. "Are you Miss Burrell?" he asked.

"Yes, I am." I smiled.

He took my bags, and I followed him to his car, while he made small talk about hoping I'd had a pleasant trip and that I would like it in Alabama. I tried to answer pleasantly, although I felt far from impressed with the South at that point.

After a distance of about five miles the car turned between two stone pillars. Oakwood at last! A few young women loitered on the porch of their dormitory, which I later learned was Irwin Hall. The relative coolness I found inside the building revived my spirits somewhat as my escort led me to the dean's quarters.

A pleasant-looking young lady came to the door and extended her hand to me and smiled.

"Miss Katrina Nesbitt," the man said, introducing the young woman. Then he turned to Katrina and added, "This is your new dean, Miss Burrell." With that he left.

Katrina struggled with my suitcases and explained to me that she had been assigned to ready my apartment while the matron finished preparation for the Sabbath meals. It was nearing sundown on Friday afternoon.

I glanced around the apartment; it seemed neat and clean, and I felt thankful.

"The shower's in here," Katrina said. "I'm sure you must feel grimy from your train ride."

I found pretty towels hanging on the racks and a new cake of soap in the soap dish. After my shower I felt as sparkling and refreshed as the apartment looked. Katrina had gone, so I unpacked my clothes and shook them out, attempting to locate something suitable for Sabbath.

Many years later some of the girls wrote down their first impressions of me. One wrote:

One afternoon when we least expected, Natelkka Burrell arrived, presenting a most cultured bearing, unsmiling, well-poised, seemingly unfriendly, stylishly dressed—including a stunning blue beret and carrying an animal cage."

A terrible first impression! The truth? Hot, tired, hungry, and just plain scared was I; never before had I been a dean or dealt with college girls. I felt like a baked Alaska in reverse—cool and collected on the outside, but steaming hot inside. Could I really do this job? I had to; God had given it to me, and I could not fail.

Actually, I had come a long way from the night I first entered this world, a tiny premature baby born without eyelashes or fingernails, and weighing in, in ounces—if anybody had bothered to weigh me. It was a miracle for me to live: God must have had a plan for my life.

A Rebel Is Born

On the night of February 8, 1895 a strong wind howled around a four-story, walk-up apartment in uptown Brooklyn. All day the snow had fallen, blanketing the tall buildings and the unyielding sidewalks with a glistening white softness. Then came sleet, making hazardous footing for the dray horses clomping over the slippery cobblestone streets.

Inside the apartment, water bubbled on a large kitchen range. Granny Allen, the midwife, moved swiftly and expertly, poised like a sturdy oak that had endured many storms. All was ready for the arrival of Alberta Dabney-Burrell's third child; the first two had died in infancy.

In due time a small, premature baby girl was born. The doctor, delayed by the storm, had not arrived, but Granny Allen knew just what to do with the tiny neonate. After lining a basket with hot-water bottles and Turkish towels, she wrapped the tiny one in sterilized cotton batting and lowered it into the basket, which she had placed on a chair close to the stove. The homemade affair served as an incubator until

17

the infant emerged to survive on her own.

It proved to be a precarious survival for this child. Like her brother and sister before her, she nearly succumbed to Death's call. For years her health remained unstable, yet her parents made no invalid of her. They did all they could to encourage her to acquire skills, to become "goal oriented," and to amount to something in life.

I was that tiny baby. As I grew older, in little-girl chats with my mother I learned some things about our family history. Unlike Alex Haley, I cannot trace my roots to Africa; yet I do know I am a fully integrated Afro-American, the result of the melting pot. I have French, African, and American blood in my veins, the American including some Indian from my paternal grand-father, who was a full-blooded Cherokee.

When I was small, people used to stare at me, trying to figure out what nationality I belonged to. I didn't fit their stereotype for a black, and often they'd ask, "What are you? Are you Jewish? You're certainly not black!"

The first time I remember being asked, "What are you?" the question surprised me so that I looked up from my play at the tall white man and replied, "I'm a little girl; can't you see?" Hands in pockets, I flung out the skirt of my blue-checkered play dress. Didn't he know boys wore pants and girls wore dresses?

Unfortunately, my father passed away when I was only three, and from that time on Mother and I struggled together to care for ourselves. I learned to take my afternoon naps on a couple of boards spread over the washtubs where Mother worked in white people's homes. I was taught not to cry or fuss, but to keep out of sight and play quietly under a table or out in the backyard of our patrons. And in spite of my poor health I continued to live.

Could this have been an answer to Mother's prayers? Or had God destined that this little rebel of His must grow up to do some special work for Him? Only time would bring the answer.

Education

To be effective even rebels need to be educated. Mother knew nothing about Locke, Froebel, Pestalozzi, or even about Ellen G. White's three-pronged system of education; but she believed in educating head, heart, and hand. Through a program of integrated example and discipline she began my education soon after I could walk. She had promised God if He let me live she would train me for Him. It proved to be a formidable task, for in spite of my physical handicaps I had a strong will which needed direction.

In our home, worship of God was very important. There were also rules that Mother set up and expected me to obey; she also taught me social amenities. "Good manners and good behavior," she drilled into me, "will take you where no amount of money can."

Church and Sunday School attendance were as much a part of our lives as daily breakfast and evening prayers. We went to revivals in our own Baptist church as well as a few in a nearby Methodist church. During my ninth summer I gave my heart to Jesus and was baptized by immersion into the Baptist church. That childhood conversion has stayed by me throughout my entire life.

On my fourth birthday Mother placed a threaded needle in my hand and said, "Telkka, you're old enough to learn to sew." A few brightly colored quilt pieces she furnished caught my interest as she patiently taught me how to put them together. By the time I turned twelve I could sew, clean house, cook, bake, and wash and iron nearly as well as my mother.

My formal education began at five years of age. Mother sent me to a kindergarten run by two sisters from our church. I especially liked the neighborhood field trips we took. On one of these we passed a Chinese laundry. Some of my friends began chanting, "Chink, Chink, Chinaman—" I joined in.

But when I told Mother that evening, she scolded me. "Never let me hear you make fun of anyone, no matter what nationality. Do you hear?"

I heard. And I learned not to follow the crowd, but to set my own values, especially where people were concerned.

It was in kindergarten that I set the goal for my life's vocation. I adored Miss Perkins, my teacher, and at home I announced to Mother, "When I grow up to be a big lady, I'm going to be a teacher just like Miss Perkins."

As I entered grade school, Mother sought the best education possible for me by enrolling me in an avant-garde public school in a primarily upper-middle-class neighborhood. We did not live in that school district, but Mother had been promised an apartment there, so she started me in this special school. Among the predominantly white pupils was a smattering of Italian and black students.

Each Monday morning in our room the teacher seated the students according to their scholastic rank from the previous week's work. My head swam with pride when, at long last, the teacher called my name first and motioned for me to take the front seat in the first row. After all the commotion settled down and everyone was seated, we heard sobs coming from the back of the room.

"What's the matter, Rosa?" the teacher asked of an oversized Italian girl who had ranked sixteenth and now sat in the back seat of row two.

"I can't—can't—see—from back—back here." Rosa sobbed.

"Change places with her, Natelkka," the teacher ordered.

Crestfallen, I reluctantly obeyed, wondering why Rosa had to have the seat of honor when she could have been moved to the front seat in another row. But I noticed that the rest of the front seats were occupied by white students. I managed to choke back my disappointment. I was too timid to protest.

At home, amidst the tears I'd held in check all day, I told Mother about it. She drew me close, which was unusual for her as she always seemed too busy for affection. "Telkka," she spoke tenderly, "you may as well get used to this. Most people don't know how nice a black child can be. You did right not to question the teacher's decision, though." Mother explained that many white people expected blacks to be stupid, dumb, ignorant, lazy, dirty, and generally no-account! "You must show them differently," she said, "by studying hard and amounting to something. You must always be well-mannered and keep your desk neat and clean; you must be unselfish and thoughtful of other children. In time," she went on, "they will see how wrong they were and be glad to accept you as their friend."

When I reached high school, Mother felt I should learn a trade, so she enrolled me in a girls' manual training school which offered several vocations. I felt miserable and unhappy there; the students were unfriendly to me, and rude and disrespectful to our instructors. Besides, I wanted to be a teacher. But Mother insisted I must be practical as well. "It's fine to be a teacher," she told me, "but you need to know a trade, too, so in summertime or when you're out of work you can still support yourself."

About two years earlier Mother and I had both joined a small Seventh-day Adventist church pastored by Elder J. K. Humphrey. The four teenage girls in the church, including myself, were deeply impressed when Elder Humphrey preached about Christian education, mentioning that it was available at South Lancaster

23

Academy in Massachusetts. We set our hearts on going there, if not right away, at least sometime.

"You know I can't afford to send you there," Mother snapped back when I first mentioned my desire to her. But she must have noticed the disappointment on my face, for she added quickly, "I'll tell you what; you may go there if you can find a job and earn the money."

That was a green light for me! I quit school in March, took a job caring for two small children and keeping their parents' apartment clean, and I saved my money.

That fall the church offered to pay my tuition at South Lancaster Academy. The money I had saved would care for my room and board. I set off for the academy in high spirits.

To save money Mother put me on a boat bound for Providence, Rhode Island. From there I would take a trolley through the New England countryside to South Lancaster. After a sleepless night on the boat, I arrived in Providence, located my trolley, and chose a window seat where, if I could stay awake, I could enjoy the scenery.

I need not have worried about staying awake, for the conductor stopped by every few miles to collect more fare. I began to worry for fear my money would give out; the purse felt slimmer and slimmer while I grew hungrier and hungrier. The lunch Mother had sent along had given out; I was afraid to spend my money to buy more because I wanted to reach my destination and not be put off in some field.

As dusk descended what a relief it was to hear the conductor shout, "South Lancaster!" Gathering my belongings, I made a hasty exit. From the light of the standing trolley I made out a deep trough used to water horses. It lay in the middle of the country road, but I circumvented it. The trolley left, and I stood in total darkness. As my eyes adjusted, I discerned the outline of a country road and in the distance a lighted building. Dragging my heavy suitcase along, I finally reached the building. It turned out to be the girls' dormitory of South Lancaster Academy.

All went well for three months. I loved my classes, my teachers, my roommate, and everything about the school. Then one morning as I entered my Bible class the teacher handed me a pink slip. It read, "You may no longer attend classes until you make arrangements with the business office." Shocked, I turned and bolted for the business office.

"Mr. Trout," I protested. "I don't understand this." He glanced briefly at my slip.

"I'm sorry, Natelkka," he said, "but we haven't had a payment from you in two months. Can you explain?"

It seemed that the church had neglected to keep its promise to pay my tuition, and the only money the school had received was my first month's tuition—plus the room, and board which I paid on my arrival. My heart sank. "Could I remain until I have time to write my mother about this?" I pleaded.

"Of course," he said kindly. "We want you to stay, but we can't operate a school with no money." He wrote a slip to readmit me to classes, and I dashed back.

At my first free moment I wrote to Mother. I don't know how she did it, but she sent the necessary money by return mail. And between her efforts and mine (working at 10¢ an hour!) we ended the year with a credit of $15. I also managed to get good grades in school.

That golden year in a Christian academy will always be a treasured memory.

Roadblocks and Detours

During the summer one of my friends from South Lancaster and I attempted to earn a scholarship by selling magazines door to door in Brooklyn. But the project failed, and I went home to be with Mother who still kept up her heavy laundering schedule. However, she often complained of aching shoulders and back. I noticed her usual soft humming of hymns as she worked grew less and less. Then one night as we walked home from church she stopped and reached out for me. Her breath came in short gasps, and I realized for the first time that Mother was really sick! I helped her home and into bed. She felt better the next morning and took up her work, but the zing she'd always had was missing.

That fall she admitted she could not help me in school, but she seemed determined to educate me. To please her, I agreed to attend a private school of dressmaking in Manhattan. After two months of this, during which I learned only the first basics of dressmaking, Mother became worse, and the doctor hospitalized her. I quit school and found work as a maid for the Doughty family; Mother had been their laundress for several years.

After Mother came home from the hospital, I continued to work for the Doughtys. I feared my school days were over, since I was now the breadwinner in our family. But one day Mother phoned me at work. "There's a special-delivery letter that has just come for you from Rachel Salisbury, your friend at South Lancaster," she said.

"Please open it, Mother, and see what is so important that she should send a special-delivery letter."

There was a silence and then Mother read: "There's a job-opening in Clinton, which is not far from South Lancaster. They want a girl to work for room and board and attend academy. I've asked the lady to hold the job open until I could contact you. Could you wire your answer?"

"I can't go and leave you, Mother. You aren't well enough to support yourself yet," I at once protested.

"I can manage," Mother insisted. "I want you to go, Telkka."

That settled it.

I had Mother send a telegram, which I followed with a letter. When school opened that year, I was back on the campus of South Lancaster Academy.

"A miracle," I thought to myself. "God must really want me to be a teacher." Here, after I finished academy, I could take what was then called the normal course. It was especially designed for church-school teachers.

The job that God had opened up for me—of that I was fully convinced—entailed housekeeping for the DeBlois family. I cooked and cleaned for them—Mrs. DeBlois, her nine-year-old daughter, four older sons, and Grand Pere, Mrs. DeBlois's eighty-two-year-old father.

Grand Pere spoke only French, and how delighted he seemed when my French classes at school enabled me to exchange a few words with him. I loved the family; they treated me as a member, not a maid, and I stayed with them four years until they moved away. By that time my schooling was nearing completion, and I knew without a doubt that I would realize my childhood dreams and become a teacher.

However, before I had finished the normal course Mother passed away, and I had to leave school. Now motherless and homeless, I made arrangements for a room with a Mrs. DeLevy, a member of our church. I'd have to work to support myself, and the Doughtys gladly offered my old job to me. Coming back home to remove my belongings to the rented room, I stopped off to visit a family Mother had interested in the church, a Mr. and Mrs. Cooper.

"What arrangements have you made for a place to live?" Mrs. Cooper asked. When I told her, she exploded, "You'll do no such thing! As good as your mother has been to us, we won't think of you living alone. You just move right in here with us; this is your home!" And so I had a new family; their daughters, Ruth, Naomi, and Esther are as close to me still as if they were my own sisters.

I worked at Doughty's until September, and with the small amount of insurance Mother left me and what I'd been able to save, I returned to South Lancaster. My teachers allowed me to make up the work I'd missed from March through May. They helped me all they could.

All went well scholastically. However, after paying my full year's tuition and reserving enough for my room, which I rented off campus, I realized I had a food allowance of only 50 cents a week! It had to do, and it did. But had it not been for occasional invitations to share a meal with friends, including the only black family in the community, Silas and Martha Mason, I might not have made it. Martha often gave me potatoes, squash, lettuce, or tomatoes from her garden. This, added to my frugal meals of Spanish peanuts, bread, a stick of butter one week and a small jar of mayonnaise the next, somehow saw me through.

But one warm Sabbath morning, sitting in church with Rachel Salisbury, after having eaten only a slice of bread spread with mayonnaise for breakfast, I began to feel sick. I rose to leave, stepped into the aisle, and fainted. When I awoke, I found myself stretched out on the lawn with Rachel bending over me, holding a pitcher of water ready to pour on me. I quickly recovered and spent the afternoon at Rachel's home under the loving care of her mother.

"Man shall not live by bread alone," the Good Book says. That year I lived by faith, believing God wanted me to teach somewhere and I must complete my training for His work. I graduated with honors and returned to New York City and to Mom and Dad Cooper.

Most of my classmates had been placed; they knew where they where going, but alas, I did not. My grades were tops, my reputation excellent, my teaching ability unquestioned. But where could I be used? There were no black Adventist schools for northern children. What few black children attended church school went with the whites. Yet I felt sure God had called me to teach. If God called men to preach, couldn't He call me to teach? I would wait for His call.

It came late in August after I had spent the summer working in a millinery shop. The letter was from the educational secretary of the Southern New England Conference, and it invited me to teach a school in Guilford, Connecticut. I'd never heard of the place, but of course I would go, no questions asked. How many grades? My hours of work? Salary? It didn't matter; God had called me, and I was ready to go.

On My Way

Mrs. Wilcox, the educational secretary, met me at the Guilford train station when I arrived on a Thursday night early in September. We drove to her home, and as we sat visiting, two little girls in pigtails knocked on the door. One appeared to be Italian and the other German, but they understood English and spoke it brokenly—when they spoke at all. Apparently they had come to look the new teacher over. But although I tried to put them at ease they soon backed out of the room shyly and ran down the porch steps.

After briefing me about the school, my pupils, and their parents, Mrs. Wilcox informed me that my salary would be $40 a month and that I was to live with a Mrs. Kleuser, one of the church members.

"Come," she said; "it's getting late, and Mrs. Kleuser is expecting you for the evening meal." My eyes widened as we drove into the yard of a large white home, which I later learned had stood for a hundred years. Inside it was very well-kept, and its owner, a German lady in a fresh white apron, greeted me pleasantly.

"Supper's on the table," she announced after a brief introduction. "You'll stay, too, Mrs. Wilcox, won't you?" It was indeed a delicious meal; German cooks are noted for that, and Mrs. Kleuser lived up to the reputation. I felt lucky to be living there.

The church was right next door, so Mrs. Kleuser and I walked over on Sabbath morning. I felt a bit disconcerted as we entered, for the singing seemed to be rather garbled. I soon learned that several different languages were being used, all to the same tune, of course. It was with relief that I saw two men rise when it was time for speaking and realized there would be an interpreter, and I would hear the sermon in English.

I'll never forget my first Communion service in that church. It took place several weeks after school had opened. Two of my little students, Rosa and Martha, sat in front of me. When Communion was announced and it was explained that the ladies would retire to the schoolroom for foot washing, I overheard Rosa whisper to Martha, "Now we can see if she's like that all over!"

I suppressed a smile. All they had ever seen of a dark-skinned person was what they saw each day of me—a face, a neck, and arms from the elbow down. However, their curiosity was not satisfied that day, for their mothers had them remain in the church while the foot washing took place.

3-G.B.R.

The school was in perfect order on that opening day in September—windows sparkling, floor swept clean, and my books arranged on my desk. I had taken time to create a welcome for the children on the bulletin board. The students began to arrive by twos and threes, curious, expectant. Since long distances separated them during the summer, they were delighted to be together again for companionship and play.

After a little time spent getting acquainted, we had our opening worship. I asked the children to help me set some goals for our school year, and then we settled down to studying. I found my first-grade students bright and eager to learn; my seventh and eighth-grade pupils no problem; but as time went on, I realized the middle grades would present the greatest challenge to me. The slow learners were there. Perhaps they had missed a good foundation in earlier years.

We had a little joke among the eighth graders. If one of them failed to turn in work on time, all I had to do was say, "That's all right. You can do that next year. I'll be so happy to have you with me next year!"

It worked every time. Before school closed for the day, the work would be on my desk, often a page or two beyond the assignment!

Our curriculum called for music, but how was I to teach it without an instrument? I asked the children to pray about it, and we mentioned it in worship. Then I took the problem to the church. Within a week a lady donated a small pump organ. My hours of piano practice paid off. I pumped away on that organ, and we practiced our do-re-mis and sang songs both new and old.

Discipline, the beginning teacher's bugbear, treated me lightly. I kept busy, and I kept each child busy. Once, when one of the larger boys who loved to tease put a baby snake in my desk drawer, I managed by supreme effort not to scream. (I was deathly afraid of snakes.) As calmly as I could I said, "Herman, this poor little snake has lost its mother. Won't you please take it outdoors so it can find her?" I was pretty sure the prank had been done by Herman or his brother, but at any rate the joke had lost its punch.

At recess time I became like a child again and ran and jumped with my children in the big cow pasture allotted to us for a playground. No child was ever out of my sight for very long.

The year rolled to its close with feelings of accomplishment by both teacher and pupils. I had learned a great deal, and my self-confidence had grown.

The board invited me to return the next year.

Back to the Pots and Pans

During the summer months after my first year of teaching I found work as cook and dishwasher at an all-girls camp, Camp Menuncatuk, on the bay about five miles from Guilford.

Mrs. Hooker, who owned the camp, hired me at my first interview and put me to work at once. God had cared for my needs; I would have more than the promised bread and water. For the summer I would live off the fat of the land!

Mrs. Hooker, a retired teacher, possessed a charisma all her own. She lived in a small white cottage at the edge of the camp, which overlooked the bay and the lighthouse.

The very first night I slept at Camp Menuncatuk Mrs. Hooker elected to sleep in a tent near me instead of in her cottage, although I didn't know it at the time.

Being fearful of snakes, I checked my tent thoroughly before retiring. I secured the tent flaps, put my flashlight under my pillow, and then crawled into bed.

A few minutes later I heard a noise outside. The tent swayed. Something brushed against the tent, and I could hear heavy breathing. I froze. What could it be? Had a fox wandered out from the woods? A deer? A bear? "No, there are no bears around here," I tried to assure myself. But again the tent swayed, this time even harder. Whatever was out there was big!

"Lord," I prayed, "whatever it is please don't let it get into this tent!" I covered my head. Plop! Plop! Plop! The sounds, grew fainter. "It's moving away! Oh, thank You, Lord." At last I fell into a fitful sleep.

Next morning I gingerly untied the tent flaps to let in the sunshine. I could see Mrs. Hooker moving about in the screened-in kitchen not far away.

"Good morning, Natelkka," she greeted me as I walked over. "Did those old cows bother you last night?"

"Is *that* what tried to knock my tent over? You came very near not having a cook," I said with a laugh. "I had decided to pack up and leave this place to the wild beasts."

My employer laughed and patted my arm. "You *are* precious," she declared. "City born and city bred."

Always mindful of snakes, I endured living in a tent all summer but was relieved to find the tents had been replaced with screened-in cottages the second summer I worked there. Mrs. Hooker furnished me with several summers of work between teaching jobs. I enjoyed the girls and the limitless supply of good food, but each fall I looked forward eagerly to returning to the classroom.

While teaching in Guilford I met some friendly people, Mr. and Mrs. Leatherberry, who operated a tailor shop along with a dry-cleaning business in downtown Guilford. I discovered that Mrs. Leatherberry kept the seventh-day Sabbath. She had no idea there were others in Guilford who believed as she did. After meeting her I invited her to attend church with me, and later, after I had moved away, she became a baptized member of the Guilford Seventh-day Adventist Church.

The Leatherberrys were blacks. There was only one other black family in the small town, and they lived in a rather run-down house on the outskirts. When I enquired about them, some of the church members said, "Oh, them. They're just no good. Drunkards of the worst sort. Better not bother with them."

Unfortunately, I took their advice and failed to contact this poor family, thus displaying my "feet of clay." Had I visited them, offered to help with the raggedy little children swarming around the tumble-down building they called home, I might have been able to lead them to Christ. I have always regretted my negligence.

My second year at Guilford went well, but I recall one incident where I feel I handled the problem in the wrong way. My first and second grade that year consisted of three lively, but well-behaved little boys. Remembering Ellen G. White's admonition that "children should be as free as little lambs until they are eight or ten years old," I conferred with my school board (mostly parents) and received permission to dismiss them from school an hour early. One boy lived within walking distance, but the other two had to wait for older brothers or sisters to finish school. I instructed the child who lived close to go home as soon as dismissed; the other two were to play quietly near my window where I could keep an eye on them.

One day after I let the three boys go, an older girl who had gone to the girls' outside privy returned and reported that the one little fellow who was to go home had not done so. She had heard the three boys giggling in the boys' privy.

I sent an older boy to retrieve the mischief makers. "Sit in your desks until school is over," I told them. "Then I will talk with you."

By questioning I found out what they had been doing. I explained why it was wrong, and they said they were sorry. We prayed about it together, and I should have let the matter drop, but I felt punishment must be severe. I spanked each of those precious little boys. Those spankings still haunt me!

At the end of the second year of teaching the Guilford School the enrollment had dwindled until the church felt it could no longer support a school. However, the Southern New England Conference contacted me with a different kind of offer. They invited me to become a Bible worker.

New Dimensions in Teaching

"Well, God, Bible work *is* teaching, I suppose; so if that's what You want me to do, I'll do my best," I said.

My assignment was with Elder Alston. Together, and with the Lord's blessing, we were to hold evangelistic meetings among the black population of New Haven and to raise up a church there. But before the summer was over, the conference realized that a church school was needed for black children, and I was hired to teach it.

Our facilities included the front of a store building the group had rented for evangelistic services, a few meager furnishings, and ten or twelve students; yet the project flourished and served to cement the new church members together with those former black members of white churches who had formed the nucleus. The little church grew.

But shortly before the school year ended, I received a letter offering me the principalship of the Baltimore Academy, an all-black school. I hardly knew how to answer. I loved the children in New Haven, yet if God was calling me to Baltimore I wanted to be willing to go.

I decided to make it a subject of prayer, and I asked for a sign. "Lord, if You are calling me to Baltimore, make them willing to pay me $75 a month." (In New Haven I was earning $50 a month.) That is the only time in my life that I made salary the decisive factor in accepting denominational work. The Baltimore Academy school board answered my letter promptly; they would pay $75 a month.

Could I have seen what lay ahead, would I have gone so willingly? Eager to try a larger school and confident that I could handle it, I packed my belongings and headed for the big city. On that first Sabbath morning as I walked down that long, narrow church aisle in the Druid Hill Church, all seemed placid enough. Elder Matthew Strachan introduced me to the congregation as the new principal, and I looked into the faces of several hundred questioning and expectant people, but I saw no expressions of friendliness on those faces.

School convened Monday morning right there in the church. The ninety-some students sat on the immovable pews, the upper grades in the front section, the middle grades at the rear while the primary grades met in the balcony. Teachers for each section set up small blackboards on a vacant pew; they had no desks or any semblance of modern teaching equipment. We all suffered from eyestrain and poor ventilation due to the immobile stained-glass windows in the church.

We could not brighten the drab tan-painted walls with pictures or put up bulletin boards to catch the children's attention. It was a deplorable setup. But those parishioners and their pastor were staunch believers in Christian education, so they did not wait for ideal conditions. They used what they had—a building, empty on week days, and a flock of children!

One kindly intentioned person informed me that my predecessor had broken under the strain of trying to control the older children. Some of the parents, I was told, had been uncooperative to the point of "beating up the principal"!

I listened, but after consulting with my other teachers, we quietly and prayerfully went about our work doing the best we could under the circumstances.

My informer had been right. Fights broke out among the older boys, many of them husky fellows accustomed to fighting their way through life. A few from the ghettos had difficulty adjusting to and understanding the more subtle ways of their middle-class schoolmates and teachers. Talking or reasoning seemed to them weakness. I had learned in my schooling no techniques for working with such children. I had to depend solely upon God. These were His children, and He knew how to handle them. God taught me how.

But children did not always cause the problems. I had to come to grips with the very grandmother who the year before had beaten up the principal. One day her grandson, William, became angry and kicked his teacher. I sent him home with a note that he could not come back to school until he brought his grandmother with him. About an hour later I was informed that Grandma was waiting for me in the vestibule. I left my classes in another teacher's care and met Grandma in the entrance to the church. Arms akimbo, eyes flashing, she confronted me. I kept my cool and informed her that no pupil would be tolerated in our school who disrespected a teacher.

"I want you to spank William here in this school, and then I will readmit him," I told her.

"I'll whup him at home," she sputtered.

"No, you'll do it here. William kicked his teacher in front of all his schoolmates. They must know you do not tolerate such behavior. They won't know it for sure if it's done at home."

Grandma tried to loud-talk me. I remained calm, keeping my voice low, but steady and positive. Finally she said, "I ain't got no strap."

"We have one," I said, handing it to her; I had taken it with me when I went to meet her. "Take it to the basement and use it on William."

She waddled down the steps with poor little William in tow. Soon we all heard the blows fall and William's ensuing screams.

"That will do," I called down authoritatively. "Bring William up here." They came back into the vestibule. "Thank you. I'll take care of William now."

I took him into the restroom, washed his face and hands, straightened his clothes, and talked

43

gently to him for a few minutes. Then I kissed him and sent him back to his teacher with the suggestion that he tell her he was sorry he had hurt her.

I had no more trouble with parents. However, I had to lecture my big boys and girls. They had ganged up with baseball bats ready to defend me had Grandma attacked me!

And so the school year rolled on. That year my teachers and I planned and executed an outstanding close-of-school program. We hired a hall, sold tickets, and cleared nearly $200 for the school. Each year following that we put on a similar program, with larger and larger audiences in attendance. We used the occasions to display the children's work and advertise the school to the public.

One such happening served to add a third dimension to my life—romance!

Romance and the Rebel

As my second year of teaching in Baltimore drew to a close, I suddenly realized we needed a large hall for the close-of-school program. I would have to see about reserving a hall at once. We would need it for two nights. The previous year we had had such a large crowd that many had had to stand and others were turned away. This year I decided to go to the Y.M.C.A. Even though I had put off finding proper accommodation for the program, I hoped that the Y.M.C.A. could help us out.

I approached the desk and found myself face-to-face with a most attractive young man—tall, keen of face, gentlemanly, and of my own race. He spoke to me in a courteous yet businesslike manner. I concluded my business, and we chatted for a few minutes. I found that he, like myself, was unmarried, not engaged, and had no "special" friend. His name was Matthew Saunders.

"May I take you out to dinner next week?" he asked.

Being quite impressed with him, I readily assented and gave him my phone number.

That night I mentioned to my landlady that I had met a very interesting young man and that he might be calling on me. Then I added, "I wish I knew more about him."

"I can find out about him from my pastor," the landlady volunteered. He works at the courthouse; he is acquainted with all the Y.M.C.A. workers."

Accordingly, a few nights later the landlady's pastor came to dinner, and when she introduced me, he asked, "Is this the young lady who wants to know about Matt Saunders?"

Embarrassed, I nodded shyly, and he continued, "You have nothing to worry about there; Matt is a fine young man, with an excellent reputation."

"Thank you, Sir," I murmured. I was proud that my judgment had been correct. Matt soon became a regular visitor, and we discovered we had many similar interests. He did not drink, smoke, or use profanity. We both loved the out-of-doors and enjoyed the same kind of music. Each of us worshiped God, but in separate denominations. We were soon deeply in love.

But, alas! Ringing through my mind was the admonition from the Bible, "Be ye not unequally yoked together." And the still sterner one from Ellen G. White, "a home where the shadows are never lifted." I struggled with the problem night after night as I tossed and turned, sleep eluding me until the wee hours of dawn.

Where could I turn for advice? My mother was

gone. My pastor wouldn't understand, I felt. I had no close friends nearby that I could trust. Anyhow, I knew what the answer would be. I had to give Matt up! I could not conscientiously marry outside of my church.

But who within the church was available? Some beardless, immature teenager? Some superannuated fossil with one foot in the grave? I asked myself. Finding no solution, I turned bitter. If I couldn't marry Matt, why didn't God provide someone suitable in the church? Had God run out of Isaacs for his Rebeccas? I had much to learn about my heavenly Father's ways in affairs of the heart.

At last one evening in the quiet of my third-floor room I came face-to-face with my personal Gethsemane. I laid the problem of my non-Adventist suitor before the Lover of my soul, and by His grace I sweat out the words, "Not my will, but Thine be done." My tears flowed freely; I wrung my hands and paced the floor until finally on bended knee I capitulated wholly to Jesus Christ.

When I told Matt I could not marry him because of our religious differences, he promised everything except to study the Adventist truths I held so dear. In the end we had to part, each deeply hurt and disappointed. Later, Matt married, and still later he became a Baptist minister. I've always wondered, Might it have been different had my light shone brighter?

In every church, it seems, there are people who are fascinated by the romances of the young; they delight in matchmaking. This happily married couple in the church seemed worried over my single blessedness. One Sabbath morning a tall, handsome black man with features as still as though carved in obsidian sat across the aisle from the two cuddly turtledoves. As soon as the service ended, the couple crossed the aisle to welcome the visitor from Africa and to introduce him to other members as they came along.

As I reached them, they practically threw me at the young man. The woman introduced me; then turning to her mate, she cooed, "Don't they look nice together?"

"Yes, Dear," the man agreed.

"Why doesn't he see her home?" the woman suggested out loud with a knowing smile.

I interrupted. "Perhaps the gentleman has other plans." I couldn't have him think I was making a play for him.

"It would be my pleasure to see Miss Bur'l home," the young man insisted promptly.

What more could I say? It was a pleasant association. He called several times, always observing the social amenities—a perfect gentleman. Then he went to Washington for a few weeks. But on the first evening after his return, he came to see me at my rooming house.

"I hear there's to be a concert in Washington next week," he told me. "Marian Anderson will be singing. I would be happy if you would be my guest."

"I'd be delighted," I assured him. "I've always

wanted to hear Marian Anderson sing."

But unfortunately when he was ready to leave that night, he attempted to kiss me. Instinctively, I drew back.

"Ah," he murmured close to my ear, "in Washington I have learned what American women like."

I pulled away still further. "I'm sorry," I told him. "All American women are not free with their kisses."

He backed away, looking shamefaced. I tried to smooth it over by bidding him a courteous "Good night," but as the week wore on with no phone call from him, my hopes of hearing Marian Anderson ebbed.

On the night of the concert, although I dressed and waited for him, just in case, the clock ticked slowly on past the hour for the concert. My landlady and I talked it over and decided I had committed the unpardonable sin so far as my African friend was concerned. I had caused him to lose face. I, an American woman, had put him down. I wrote him off.

It was strange, though. This handsome African not only vanished from my life, he also vanished from the church. I never saw him again.

"I, Natelkka, Take This Man"

After I had taught two years in the Baltimore school, the church purchased a much larger and more commodious building with special classrooms. This greatly increased expenses, so as a fund-raising project the church opened a lunchroom. Usually, I escaped the sweltering heat of the asphalt city streets by returning to the coolness of Connecticut's Camp Menuncatuk. But the summer the lunchroom opened I stayed on as cook, waitress, and general manager. Mr. Bishop, the head trustee of the church, and a very successful businessman, did the buying and managed the money.

Since I worked until ten o'clock at night, a time too dangerous for me to walk home with the day's receipts, Mr. Bishop always came in an hour or so before closing time to help clean up and set things in order for the next day. Then he'd count the day's receipts and leave enough in the cash register with which to start the next day, lock up, and drive me home. Out of these contacts a friendship grew.

One radiant Sunday afternoon when I didn't

50

have to work, "Bish," as we called him, asked, "How would you like to take a drive around the city with me?"

"I'd be delighted," I told him, and we were soon on our way. By way of conversation he asked, "How do you like our city?"

"I don't know," I answered. "All I've seen is these row on row of all-alike houses with their white marble steps. Is there more to Baltimore?"

He laughed and said, "I see I'll have to show you the real Baltimore." He drove through more affluent neighborhoods and finally into an inviting park where we strolled under the shade trees. In the weeks to come we often visited that park, always with pleasure. The drives we took convinced me that Baltimore was indeed a very nice city after all.

On a later day that summer, after another drive, we stood looking at some water lilies growing in a quiet pond in "our" park. Not a breeze stirred; not a bird called. In this garden setting Joseph H. Bishop asked me to be his wife. I consented.

Since I had promised to continue as principal for another school year, Bish and I decided not to announce our engagement until the school year was nearly over. But church people are curious, and Bish's extra attentiveness to me made questions fly. "Are the principal and the head trustee going together?" "Are they in love?" "Is she really going to marry him?"

Finally the guessing contest grew too strong. The pastor came to call on me and asked, "Are you thinking of marrying Mr. Bishop?"

"Thinking about it? Well, yes, I am." I smiled.

At once the minister began to protest. "He's too old for you. God wants you to marry a minister. Anyway, you don't know this man well enough; he's just not right for you!"

I took his objections one by one. "I know Mr. Bishop is years older than I. But he's an intelligent Seventh-day Adventist Christian." I paused. "As for your second suggestion—that I marry a minister—I have never wanted to do that." I parried the third objection with a question, "What do you know about Mr. Bishop that impels you to tell me he is not right for me? He's apparently your closest friend; don't you believe in his integrity?"

The pastor never answered my question. But he offered instead to help me find a suitable husband. I thanked him, but declined his offer emphatically.

When school closed, I left immediately for my summer job at Camp Menuncatuk along the seashore in Connecticut. I knew I had left a young, non-Adventist rival named Sally for my fiance's affections.

Bish owned and operated a first-class beauty salon, and Sally was one of his best operators. She pursued him relentlessly. I thought Bish should be left to make up his own mind, and I wrote him to that effect. I assured him there would be no hard feelings if he chose to break our engagement. His letter in return emphatically denied any such desire, and he also told me that Sally was not working for him anymore.

At the end of the summer we consummated our wedding plans. Bish would drive up to New Haven, where I would meet him and show him the way to the camp. On the day he was to arrive I took the trolley and rode sixteen miles to New Haven, eagerly looking forward to beholding the face of the man to whom I'd promised to commit my life. As we had agreed, I went to the train station to meet him. I waited and waited. More than two hours passed. Where could he be? Had Sally won out after all? Or had he been in an accident? A large sign flashing overhead in the waiting room caught my attention:

WILL NATELKKA BURRELL COME
TO THE INFORMATION DESK
IMMEDIATELY, PLEASE.

With a sense of alarm and dread I made myself known at the desk and was given the following message: "I'm waiting in the train station in Guilford. J.H.B." In his eagerness, Bish had forgotten to stop in New Haven and had gone straight on to Guilford! What a relief! At least he was not hurt. I spent another hour rocking along in the old trolley back to Guilford before we were clasped in each others arms. Our wedding day lay ahead!

After catching up on the news, we made our way to his car and drove out to camp in happy anticipation.

The next day, my summer's job ended, we picked up two friends for witnesses and drove back to New Haven for the ceremony. We had previously arranged for the young pastor of the New Haven Front Street Church to marry us, so we met him at the courthouse that morning and took our vows.

After the pastor had pronounced us husband and wife, we bade our friends and the minister good-bye and drove back to Camp Menuncatuk where Mrs. Hooker awaited us with a surprise wedding breakfast. Our two-day honeymoon at camp among the tall trees and along the sandy beach of the bay came to an end all too soon, and we had to head back to Baltimore and its crowded row-on-row houses.

The Serpent Enters

The long drive from Connecticut to Baltimore finally ended; Bish stopped the car in front of our home. Store lights blazed. Neighbors, clerks, and some of Bish's beauty operators, along with a few church members, waited to welcome the bride and groom. When congratulations, good wishes, and teasing finally ceased, Bish and I went upstairs to our four-room apartment, tired but happy.

Bish's trade included a full line of hair and beauty preparations which he sold wholesale. He also operated the ten-booth beauty salon underneath our apartment and a retail store for his products, beauty-shop furniture, and all appurtenances of the trade.

My new husband was a delightful person to live with, tender, loving, and most considerate. Our lives soon settled into a regular pattern, with Bish on the road selling much of the time, while I was in charge of the business at home. As a teenager I had received some training as a beauty operator, so managing the shop posed no problem. I kept busy and business increased.

We closed our shop from sundown Friday

until sundown Saturday night, but took some appointments through the evening on Saturday. We attended church each Sabbath, paid a faithful tithe, and gave at least a token to the various enterprises of the church. However, we no longer were offered any offices in the church. There seemed to be a coolness in the church's attitude toward us. We accepted this without too much concern. We had each other and life was good, so why did we need work in the church?

Perhaps it was at this point our communication began to break down. Bish was a man of few words, and I had been used to managing my own life so long that I kept my opinions to myself.

In questioning some of my friends, later in our marriage, I learned that Bish, before our marriage, had been living with a woman not his wife. I never could figure out why, at the time I was dating him, he held an important office in the church, but later after we were married, the attitude of the church changed. I should have discussed this with Bish, but my lifelong habit of keeping my problems to myself surfaced, and I pushed it out of my mind.

Bish and I had a satisfactory financial arrangement. For my assistance in the store and beauty salon he gave me half of all the money I earned in the salon. On good days I often cleared twenty-five or thirty dollars, and fifteen dollars a day free and clear was good pay for the 1920s and early 30s. I gave good service. Customers liked me and trade boomed.

Bish would never lead out in family worship, and I felt timid. I did suggest opening the Sabbath each week with prayer. He cooperated, but left me with the impression that his heart wasn't in it; he was merely humoring me. I enjoyed playing hymns on my piano and singing. Bish would listen, nod agreement to my comments on the message of the hymn, but never add any himself, nor did he join me in singing.

"You know I have no singing voice, Natelkka," he told me, so I quit urging him to take part in my singing, and gradually our weekend worships ceased.

So far as I could see, Bish had only one bad habit, his early-morning cup of coffee. He brewed it himself, saying he had to have it to get started.

"God doesn't want you to put that poison in your body, Bish." I remonstrated. "You know it's against our beliefs."

He never answered me, but the next morning he would brew his coffee as usual. I prayed for him to overcome this bad habit, but always in secret. We never argued over anything. In fact we grew less communicative with each other due to our work keeping us apart much of the time. After his morning coffee, Bish would rush downstairs to his office; he seldom came back for breakfast. I always prepared dinner, but we seldom ate it together, except on weekends.

I don't know how it happened, but we both began to lose interest in the church. No one seemed to care. Our attendance became sporadic, and our tithe and offerings followed suit. When I attended church alone, people seldom asked about my husband's absence.

After a full day's work neither Bish nor I felt like talking; we had been dealing with people all day. It was much easier to simply exchange a few words, usually about the business, and fall asleep. Bish trusted me implicitly; I knew the combination to the safe and the secret of his formula, but I did not know what went on in his head. I simply did not know how to draw him out. Since I had grown up alone, with a mother who allowed no demonstration of affection, I'd never learned how to use kisses and hugs to wheedle information out of one I loved. There was no drastic change in Bish's manner toward me at first, just a gradual withdrawal, and I couldn't figure out why, since our physical life together was still normal.

Bish began to take weekend trips to New York. Finally, he decided to open the beauty salon on Sabbaths, which at first shocked me, but finally I went along with the idea. I had completely lost faith in the church and no longer attended or paid tithe. Once earlier, I had asked for help from our young minister.

"You haven't put any money in the church, Sister Bishop," he said, and I turned away completely crushed. I never told Bish about it.

Because of the business it was difficult for Bish and me to get away together. Once Bish suggested that I take a vacation at the seashore.

"You look pale, Natelkka. You've been working pretty hard," he told me. "I wish I could join you, but you know we can't both leave at the same time."

I was touched by his concern and readily accepted his suggestion. He drove me over, rented a cottage, and said he would be back for me in a week. I took long walks along the beach, lay in the sun, and took an occasional dip in the ocean. I felt lonely, but I trusted Bish; it never entered my head that he might be using the week to satisfy his own desires. I returned at the end of the week, refreshed and ready for more hard work.

Sally must have reentered the picture during the time I spent at the seashore. I found some of her clothing in my bureau drawer and in the closet. Without a word I held them out to Bish.

"Oh," he laughed, with no show of embarrassment. "One of the girls must have come up here to change before going home." I didn't press him, but I didn't believe his story. I hid the clothes; I knew if they belonged to one of our operators she'd soon ask for them. Besides, I knew beauticians didn't wear nightgowns to work.

In a few days the clothes disappeared from the hiding place. Bish must have taken them back to Sally. I should have vented my disappointment in him and had it out at that time, but I said no more to him about the incident. Even with such evidence, I wondered what could be happening to us, and a few days later I said to Bish, "We really need to talk."

"About what?" he snapped.

"About us."

"Us?"

"Yes, what is happening? Are you upset with me? Have I done something to offend you?"

"No," he answered quickly and went downstairs into the office. A short time later I heard him go out. That night he came home drunk. This soon became his usual pattern, and I suffered in silence, too brokenhearted to pursue the matter.

I tried to turn back to God. I prayed for forgiveness of my own waywardness and for strength to endure and wisdom to understand, but it seemed God wasn't answering just then. I prayed that God would reach my husband, whom I still loved dearly; I begged God to protect him when he drove while half drunk. Our business began to fail; I prayed that it would revive and that we would have more sales so Bish would be happy.

In January of our third year of marriage, I was rushed to the hospital for emergency surgery. Bish was drinking heavily by then, but he came to the hospital every day to see me.

The business dwindled, and bills piled up. When I returned home, I soon took up my duties again. But I could not save the business. Bish took all the cash from the register every night and then took off, returning in the wee hours of the morning, usually dead drunk.

The first night he had come home late like that I was frantic. I knew he had the car and probably was drinking. All I could think of was that he lay in some hospital or, worse, in some morgue. Finally I called the police station in our district. They assured me no accident had been reported.

"Don't worry," the policeman told me. "He'll come home eventually."

He did—at three in the morning. He was so drunk I got only a blurred answer to my question. "Where were you? I was so worried."

"Jes over't the hotel talkin'," he replied.

It was not until later that I learned that Sally had taken a room at the hotel. However, at the time I was only concerned about my husband's drinking.

After weeks of this kind of behavior, I finally made up my mind it was useless to sit up and wait for him to come home. No need of both of us going sleepless, I thought.

One night I awakened to find Bish standing over me with the loaded Colt in his hand.

"You don't do a _____ thing but sleep!" he exploded, adding a cuss word.

I became angry. "What am I supposed to do at this hour of the morning?" I retorted. Then sorry for my outburst, I got up and helped him undress for bed.

I marveled at how he could get up and function courteously all the next day in meeting customers. His drinking continued and became even worse. One evening before the store closed, he came home led by a blind man. Our office girl thought it very funny; I hurt. How could this fine, upright man I had married have allowed himself to sink so low? It didn't seem possible. Where was God? Why didn't He stop him? Why didn't He tell me how to help stop him?

One night, home early and sober for once, Bish said, "Baby, do you see that bright light?" He pointed to the window.

"No," I replied. "I don't see any light except the street light."

"That's not it," he answered impatiently. "Look! It's there in the window. It's the same light I saw the night I was nearly run over by a freight train long, long ago. That's my light. I'm following it."

I had no idea what he meant. It gave me an eerie feeling, as though evil dwelt in the room with us. But I told him, "You must have been dreaming; there isn't any light there. Go to sleep."

"God, protect us," I prayed silently.

I knew I needed to return to God. The next Sabbath I took my Bible and walked to church; Bish went into the salon to check on the girls.

How I needed the church members at that time, but they were all cool to me. The following Sabbath I took my Bible and walked to a nearby park, where I spent the morning. I prayed for my husband and for myself; I desperately wanted us to straighten out our lives and return to God, but I couldn't talk to Bish about it. I seemed to have to suffer in silence, even from God, and I had no human friends to turn to; I was into something over my head, and I had no idea how to deal with it.

One night when Bish came home rather early, fairly sober, he found me crying. It must have surprised him, for he said, "Well, now you really can feel. I didn't think you could."

I didn't blame my husband for our predicament. I decided it was my own lack of understanding of men in general and of my husband in particular. I disliked any type of confrontation; I had been brought up to control my emotions. Don't cry. Don't answer back. Don't quarrel; it's belittling. Speak softly; don't raise your voice in anger. These principles had been drilled into me from babyhood.

Bish met and made friends with the Donaldsons, a couple who were some kind of medicine hawkers and so-called healers. He joined up with the Donaldsons, rented a store a few blocks away, and hired a fortune-teller. The fortune-teller and Bish lured customers into the store and sold them on the liniment Bish had invented along with what the Donaldsons sold. This partnership evolved into an experiment with spiritualism. The atmosphere in our home became saturated with evil spirits. Bish would send his mediums in to meet me. One of them told me on her first visit, "You are surrounded by evil spirits. I can feel them." I knew that. I also knew only God could deal with them, and I prayed that He would. I did not feel welcome in the white church, and there was no black church near to which I could turn. Life seemed not worth living.

Good-bye to Marriage

"I've just put a new operator into the beauty shop," Bish informed me one morning after he had downed his cup of coffee. Several had quit, so I wasn't surprised.

"Fine," I answered. "What's her name?"

He was halfway down the stairs by this time, but he flung back at me, "Sally" and disappeared into the shop.

Sally! The girl who had threatened our engagement period, the girl whose clothes I had found in my bedroom. So, she had not only moved into the hotel nearby, she now held forth in our beauty parlor. Of course Bish must have wanted her there; perhaps he wanted me to move out. I knew Sally was a good beautician, but did he have to flaunt her right under my nose?

With difficulty, I regained my composure, at least on the surface and went down to my office in the shop. I prayed for grace to treat Sally fairly.

She was on duty in booth number 4. I said good morning to all the operators, as usual, and stopped at Sally's booth.

"Welcome to our shop, Sally," I forced myself to be cheerful. "Have you met the other girls?"

"Yes. Mr. Bishop introduced me this morning," she grinned.

"I understand you've worked here before. Can you find everything you need?"

"Oh, yes. Mr. Bishop showed me where everything is last night. He gave me a private tour of the shop."

"Fine," I answered, controlling myself. "I hope you get along all right."

"I will. I always do." She muffled a giggle. I felt mortified, and seething with anger, I barely controlled myself until I had escaped into my office. I tried to concentrate on accounts, but Sally's giggle and remarks kept running through my head. What could she have meant? I suppose I knew; I just didn't want to face facts.

At suppertime I confronted my husband. "Why did you have to hire Sally? There are plenty of other operators around."

"Sure. But she's worked for me before, and I know she's a good operator. I'm sure she'll be an asset to the business."

Suddenly I lost control. "Business! Business! But what about our marriage?" I shouted. Stammering, I tried to tell him how I felt threatened with Sally working down there, but I could not put it into words. Bish simply shrugged his shoulders, pushed back from the table and walked out.

From then on we had no unpleasant words; we barely spoke at all. We presented a facade of

65

a successful marriage to the few friends we still had, but in truth our marriage had died.

The businesses were dying too. As the Great Depression of the early thirties began to creep over the nation, small businesses suffered the brunt. Creditors pressed Bish on every side. In spite of the hours he added to his beauty salon and shop, receipts fell off until his cash flow became inadequate.

Lower income and pressing creditors called for greater activity, my husband seemed to reason. He tried to ease his worries with alcohol, and he played the horses for money. On several occasions when it came time to pay the girls I had to dip into my personal savings, because Bish had stripped the cash register and safe.

Naturally, all this affected me adversely. It is painful to watch the destruction of all that is good in a man, and of course I kept questioning, Why is all this happening to me? Could it be my fault? I didn't know what to do about it. I still loved the *memory* of the man I had married, but he seemed like a stranger to me now. "God," I cried out from my lonely bed night after night, "can't You help me? Can't You help Bish not to completely destroy himself?"

As I came down the stairs one evening to the office, my husband jumped up and faced me with his Colt .45 again. I hadn't known he was there, and I backed away from him.

"I could kill you!" he shouted. "They wouldn't do anything to me; I'm a 32nd degree Mason."

I told him to go ahead; I wasn't going anywhere. But he put up the weapon and said, "I'm not going to kill you." He walked out of the office door and down the street.

And then, of course, there was Sally. As the weeks and months dragged by, she became bolder and bolder, flaunting her position as "the other woman." Things came to a head one night in the beauty shop. The other girls had gone home; we were closing, and I spoke to Sally for the third time about something she insisted on leaving undone. She answered me disrespectfully. With an effort, I remained cool and spoke quietly but firmly.

"Sally, you may be running with my husband, but I am still married to him. You know the rules of the shop; he made them, and I am here to enforce them!"

She turned sharply to face me. "Yes, I'm running with your husband, and I haven't just started, either!"

My nerves snapped. I raised my hand and smacked her hard; then I left her and walked into my office. Sally left without a good-bye. When Bish came home, I told him what I had done and why. "If you ever bring that woman into this place again, I'll kill her." I hissed. "I mean that!"

He stared at me a minute, then tried to pacify me by saying, "Let's talk about that tomorrow, Baby."

"No!" I snapped. "We may both be dead tomorrow." Startled, he stepped closer. "Baby, Baby, you don't talk like that!"

"No, I don't," I retorted, "but it's high time I did. My Indian blood is boiling. I can kill if I have to sit in jail forever. It's up to you. Bring her in; I'll kill her!"

The next day Sally's booth was empty.

I sensed I had gone too far, that Bish really wanted Sally in his shop and in his life. Only one solution came to me. Walk out. I did it.

I found a room in a good neighborhood, and the landlady lent a willing ear to my troubles, although I didn't burden her with the full load. She extended credit to me until I could find a job, and later we became very close friends. She suggested I call her Mama Scott, as she was old enough to be my mother, and Mama Scott she has been to me all the rest of my life.

The Adjustment

It took several days for me to relax and settle down in my new location, but at last my nerves began to unwind. My next need, I realized, was a job. Three years earlier I had passed the Maryland Teacher's Exam and had been accepted as a substitute teacher. After leaving my husband I could have had it reactivated, but I felt too nervous and shaky to deal with children just then. I decided to look for work as a domestic helper.

I bought a newspaper and scanned the ads, praying that God would help me. I wondered time after time if I had done the wrong thing in leaving Bish. He had not tried to contact me, although at least a few of my friends knew where I was staying. When I called the phone number on one of the ads, a lady answered.

"Do you do laundry?" she asked.

"Yes."

"Are you a good cook? Do you mind a couple of school-age children? I answered Yes to the first and No to the second question. Then she asked, "Are you married?"

"Yes, I am, but—"

"Sorry. We don't want a married woman." The receiver clicked. I decided from then on my name would be Miss Burrell for work purposes.

A young girl who worked assembling pages for wallpaper books told me of an opening where she worked. I got the job. But I didn't like it, so a few weeks later I applied for work with a weekly newspaper. I was accepted as a typist. Each week I typed labels for the mailing list, added new names as subscriptions came in the mail, and on Thursday night I helped "put the paper to bed." We folded the paper, wrapped it, and put a label on each paper ready for delivery to the post office. That left very little to do Friday mornings.

One Friday morning I awoke feeling extremely tired. As I started to bathe, every spot I touched felt sore; I began to feel sick. I'll just go back to bed until noon, I decided; then I'll go to work for the afternoon shift. But after a short sleep I awoke aching all over. Mama Scott insisted on calling a docter. He diagnosed my illness as rheumatic fever and recommended hospitalization.

Mama Scott, bending over my bed to stroke my feverish forehead, declared, "She don't have to go to no hospital if you'll let me take care of her here, Doctor." She must have read the reluctance in my eyes, bless her! The doctor agreed, gave Mama Scott instructions, and sent a visiting nurse in each day to care for me. I couldn't feed myself or brush my hair for several weeks; it took three months for me to regain my strength and begin minimal care of myself. After the fever left me I had plenty of time to think, pray, and attempt to put my life in shape again.

One morning Mama Scott came into my room with her usual smile. "A letter for you," she said, holding a letter out to me.

Eagerly I tore open the envelope, opened the folded sheet, and noted the signature.

"Why it's from Pastor and Mrs. Strachan," I declared. "He pastored the church in Baltimore when I was principal of the academy." Scanning the page, I said, "They're living in New York now, and listen to this!" I quoted some of the letter.

" 'You must come and join us, Natelkka. We've heard about your illness, and I am a nurse. I can give you hot packs and massages, and we'll soon have you on your feet.' "

As soon as my doctor gave his consent, I left for New York. Mama Scott promised to write and keep in touch with me, and she did. Mrs. Strachan, true to her word, treated me with hot packs and soothing massages, and my body responded to her faithful care. More important, my soul responded to Pastor Strachan's healing balm as he studied the Word of God daily with me. God had not forgotten His wavering rebel; once more my feet were being planted on the right track.

While I stayed with the Strachans, word came to them that my husband had died in a Philadelphia hospital; the funeral was set for a few days later. Mrs. Strachan insisted that I go and offered to go with me, which I greatly appreciated.

In the mortuary Bish's body lay in an oak casket. My eyes filled with tears as I gazed upon the remains of my once robust husband. What had caused his death, I wondered. An accident? An illness? No one was around to tell me. Only one floral piece graced the top of the casket; I felt a tinge of regret that I had not thought to send one. I assumed Sally had sent that one floral piece. She and a lady friend seemed to be the only mourners. The mortician spoke briefly. There were no eulogies, no telegrams, nothing. I felt numb, removed both in spirit and in body from this man who had once been my husband, this man who had once been a child of God. If only Bish had remained faithful to his God, how different our lives might have been. I wiped a few tears from my eyes, my last tribute to the man Joseph H. Bishop had once been.

Sally invited us to go to the cemetery with her, but I declined; I could not pretend a friendship I did not feel. For me that day closed a chapter in my life. But not quite; it took a few more weeks of adjustment. I had never hated my husband, just felt sorry for him and for the way he had wounded me, and, perhaps, for the way I had somehow failed him. But I still harbored hatred in my heart for Sally, and I knew God required me to love her.

As my heart and body healed, I requested re-baptism. I came out of the water once again, hoping to walk with God forever. But one more thing I felt God must do for me—help me to forgive Sally. I prayed that He would; it didn't happen overnight, but the day finally came when my tears flowed for Sally and all my anger washed away. Wherever she may be, I hope God has forgiven Sally and saved her soul. And I thank Him for cleansing me and making me whole again, though I will bear the scars of my unsuccessful marriage forever.

My Return to Teaching

Except for a slight limp and a few scattered memories—both bitter and sweet—I recovered from my physical and emotional maladies. It was time for me to go back to work.

Elder Strachan recommended me to the Ephesus Church Board to teach grades seven and eight in the Harlem Academy. And they hired me.

Two blocks from the school I found a place to live in Club Caroline, a home for business women similar to Y.W.C.A.

I enjoyed the camaraderie that existed among the teachers in the academy. And what a delight to teach those junior high-school youth. Their questioning of life and their zest for living intrigued me. Their newfound maturity still encompassed by the eggshell of childhood, yet bursting forth into all kinds of exciting possibilities gave me an incentive for meeting each new day. What would the day bring forth?

During my four years at Harlem Academy I learned the meaning of mainstreaming—the practice of placing disadvantaged children in the same grade with their normal classmates and letting the teacher worry about the problems. Among my classes at different times I had children crippled with birth defects, two with weak hearts, several with poor vision and/or hearing problems, a stutterer, and an occasional lazy learner who could do the work but wouldn't unless pushed into it. I helped the children who were normal to feel a responsibility toward their less-fortunate classmates and to try to help them rather than poke fun at them.

Eventually, I fell into the position of being called on by the teachers of the elementary grades for help in solving their problems. I learned to know all the children and enjoyed figuring out what to do about Suzy's tardinesses, Joe's disinterest in reading, and Eliza's poor grades in math. Then there were hungry children from poverty-stricken homes, improper practices in certain neighborhoods harmful to the children, and little children too young to go home by themselves while their parents both worked and couldn't come for them. Such problems-solutions I added to my teaching load. To me, teaching involved so much more than "readin', ritin' and 'rithmetic."

Church-school teachers still received meager salaries—women more so than men. With the closest budgeting I could not make nine months' pay stretch over twelve months. For two summers more I returned to Camp Menuncatuk.

The following summer a friend I had made at Club Caroline, suggested I apply for a job with the family for whom she worked in Red Bank, New Jersey. Katie had the job of cooking for the Rossis.

Mrs. Rossi hired me immediately as a second girl and laundress. When summer ended, they tried to persuade me to continue with them in their New York City apartment. They paid excellent wages. There would be comfortable living quarters for me, and the work would be fairly easy.

The idea tempted me, but actually I wanted to teach more than anything else. So I returned to Harlem Academy for my fourth year.

At the end of the school year the church members felt they could no longer support the school as an academy. They decided to cut back to eight grades. They hoped I would stay on. They planned to hire a husband-wife team, the wife to teach and the husband to look after the janitor work at the church and school. Living quarters would be provided for the three of us at the school. A thin partition would divide our living space. But since I could not feel free to live in such an arrangement, I declined the position.

Before long an opportunity presented itself to me to teach on Long Island. A former teacher, Elise Perkins, at the Harlem Academy had opened a small business school in her home. She invited me to live with her and teach English and business math for her. There I spent a happy time teaching with my friend.

When enrollment dwindled to a trickle, due to the inroads of the continuing depression, I tried out for a job with the city of New York. The influx of applicants for welfare made many openings there for clerical help. I passed the typing test and was immediately assigned to District Office #28 in Harlem.

My supervisor, a Jewish women named Rose, was very amiable and easy to work for. But after spending a few days answering telephones and clearing new cases with other social agencies, as I bent over my desk Rose came to me and asked, "How were you classified?"

Fearing for my job, I answered, "As a typist. Why?"

She bent lower and whispered, "Go to the office and get them to change it to clerk. There's no advancement as a typist, and you're too good to be stalemated here."

My fears vanished. I thanked her and took her advice. Due to her kind tip, I spent four happy years working as a clerk for the city, and I received four promotions with accompanying raises in salary during the time I worked there.

Bringing home this ever-growing paycheck enabled me to rent and furnish an apartment and to realize one of my lifelong dreams—to own a cat. I named him La Chat.

Another goal I hoped to realize was to earn my bachelor's degree, so I checked into enrolling for evening classes at Hunter College nearby. However, after receiving my transcript from South Lancaster, the registrar informed me they could not take me because South Lancaster Academy was not an accredited junior college at the time I graduated in 1917. "You will have to sit for a college-entrance exam," she told me, "covering all your high-school subjects."

How could I ever expect to pass such an exam in the 1930s when the subjects covered had been studied nearly twenty years before?

I tried to attend evening classes at a local high school with the idea of brushing up so I could pass that exam. But it was too much, and my health suffered. Each time I tried to study I would fall asleep. I finally gave up; it seemed that I'd never get that college degree.

In some classes I audited at New York University and Columbia University, just for the fun of it, I did well. Then I learned that Annett Wolter would be opening an evening class in speech and diction at reduced rates for a limited number of black students. I joined immediately. I studied under Mme. Wolter until I earned diplomas in speech and international phonetics and in dramatic art for teachers on June 15, 1938. These have proven to be of value to me in later years as I worked with both children and adults in speech and reading classes.

I really felt very self-sufficient as I completed those classes and worked for the city of New York. No clouds in my sky! I still asked God to help me do my work well and thanked Him for success, but I no longer thought of my work in terms of advancing God's kingdom. In a way my work did help people, but supervising dictaphone operators and case-history typists did little to point souls to Christ.

Then came a fiat from city headquarters: "Only civil service employees are to work in the Department of Public Welfare." For hundreds of us the nice job ended. God had slipped a worrisome pebble into my smooth life-gears.

About the same time Mme. Wolter's receptionist quit. My problem was solved; Madame offered me the job. Instead of riding a trolley or walking from my 148th Street apartment to 124th Street for my city job, I now boarded the subway en route to Mme. Wolter's Carnegie Hall studio.

But I soon learned why the previous receptionist had given up the job. In the classroom Mme. Wolter could be a delight; but at work she was a Simon Legree! I endured it for three months, then, in spite of the scarcity of jobs, I also quit. I longed to open a studio of my own, but the times forbade it. What could I do? Would I have to join the lines of suppliants for home relief? Almost defiantly, I took my problem to God. His answer: "You can teach church school." God had led me patiently along the road to the particular spot in His vineyard where He planned for me to labor.

He guided me, wide-eyed and unbelieving, into a new and an untried area of teaching. As I clung tremblingly to His steady hand, my heavenly Father steered me through the frightening waters of the Jordan River to my earthly "promised land"—a position on the staff of Oakwood College, an all-black Seventh-day Adventist College in the deep South. It proved to be the most challenging and rewarding of all my teaching experiences up to that date. God could still use a rebel like me, and my temporary lack of faith had not banished me to "forty years in the desert," as it had my ancestors, the Israelites, in Bible times.

Changing Gears for College

The challenge of Oakwood College campus rose to meet me almost at once. As I opened the doors of my private apartment and walked through the halls of the dormitory, welcomed now and then by a shy, reserved smile from one of the girls, I realized these were not only floundering teenagers of academy age, but also young maturing women attending a Christian college in search of a life vocation and perhaps more important (to them) a life companion. Instinctively, I knew I must shift gears. I must rise to meet them on their own level.

Lying awake in my room that night, after being introduced at supper as the new dean of women, I prayed that God would use me in a special way to reach these girls. My first aim, I felt, would be to establish empathy. I wanted to be three things: a Christian guide with whom to counsel and pray, a teacher with whom to learn and to grow, and at times a mother with whom to laugh, love and/or cry.

Searching back through my own experience in growing up, I recalled how my own mother had prayerfully guided me through my early life. All I really had accomplished so far in life, I realized as I lay there, I owed to my godly mother. I wanted to be to my girls what she had been to me, a steadying hand in a tumultous sea. Could I do it?

In the days that followed I sought God's help daily to enable me to handle problems wisely and to plan preventative programs which would reduce the number of discipline problems "we" (God and I) must meet.

While I believed in rules and regulations and their enforcement, I did not think a dormitory should be ruled like an army camp. Gradually, I introduced changes, some of which shocked a few faculty members. My attitude and methods of dealing with my young women soon opened new vistas in the lives of many of them. As written to me in later years, they remember:

"I found that this person that I had classed as a monster was really a human being with a lot of affection, tenderness, sympathy, and understanding," wrote one.

"In her worship talks 'Mommie' tried to give us the benefit of her training in drama. She instructed us in walking, sitting, dressing properly, conversation, and in entering a room. . . . All these things were new to me, and fascinating. I thought about them a great deal. One night after everyone was in bed, I crept downstairs to her apartment. . . . I knew there were things missing in my upbringing . . . . I asked whether she would please teach me these things. She graciously accepted the task," wrote another.

Still another student reminiscing of that year wrote:

"She spent much of her time teaching us social and cultural amenities. . . . We chose colors which complimented our skin tones and complexions. We began to watch our grammar and diction, and we used better English even in the dormitory. Our self-image began to soar. . . . Above all we were challenged to develop our talents and use them to the glory of God in helping to spread the Adventist message to the four corners of the earth.

"We didn't forget to give God the glory for sending Miss Burrell to be our dean. We realized that through her efforts, leadership, and love we were becoming thinking women with positive self-images."

The year ended. I left for summer school at Emmanuel Missionary College (now Andrews University) hoping to increase my skills as a dean and at the same time, after a hiatus of twenty-three years, continue work for my first degree. Dean Rachel Christman gave me much help that summer. Eagerly I awaited the time to return to Oakwood and "my girls." But a letter from President Moran toward the end of the summer advised me that since sickness prevented the head of the education department from continuing her post in September, I had been chosen to take her place.

I didn't want that job. The rebel in me almost surfaced.

Building a Department

When I returned to Oakwood, I moved into new quarters on the second floor of East Hall, the home for single, female teachers. I plunged immediately into preparation for my new post. No guidance was offered me from either the president or the dean of the college, so I decided to follow the existing program for teacher training. But I soon discovered what I considered weaknesses in the program.

At that time the school drew largely on General Conference funds for operating, rather than soliciting money from the constituency. Too little money flowed through our department to create a competent program so that our graduates would be qualified to teach anywhere. Oakwood catered to blacks only, and many of our students felt that by choosing to come to Oakwood little would be expected of them scholastically.

However I, along with some of the other teachers, felt strongly that students should earn grades, not be given them out of sympathy, pity, or favoritism. Eventually we got this idea across, and all students who sat under me realized it. They branded me as "hard, but just."

Since Oakwood's students came from every state in the Union, as well as from Canada and the Caribbean, its graduates should be sent out into all these areas. I felt that our education majors should be qualified to meet the requirements of any state or country, so I made a study of the offerings in selected colleges and universities, secular and denominational, from every section of the United States. Then I systematically studied Mrs. E. G. White's writings on education. Guided by this research, I constructed a new curriculum for teacher education at Oakwood College.

Problems arose in carrying out the program. However, with the laboratory teacher's cooperation, I was successful in implementing it, although it meant many extra hours of work. At one time I carried a teaching load for twenty-two hours. We could not afford to hire more teachers, so I taught art and music in the elementary school and, until Madge Douglas, one of the elementary teachers took over for me, physical education. These, of course, were in addition to all the basic methods courses. Then there was the course in Seventh-day Adventist philosophy of education and another in general psychology, required courses for teachers.

For variety I went every day to my office in the laboratory school building. As principal, I supervised its program, held meetings with its teachers, on occasion handled a disciplinary problem, and each day I spent a little time in every room observing the children at their lessons and also how my student teachers handled things.

Training ministers and church-school teachers had for many years been Oakwood's major objective. But one day in the late 40s one of my student teachers showed an unusually lax attitude toward what I had tried to teach her.

"Rosie," I spoke to her in my office, "Why aren't you more interested in learning to be an effective teacher?"

Her big brown eyes rolled toward me as she turned her hands palms-up in a typical gesture of despair. "Miss Burrell," she sighed, "why should I learn to teach? I'll be sent to one of those backwoods, one-room schools with a dozen or less students who don't even know their ABC's. So why should I learn all these interesting things you are teaching us? I won't have time to spend with those dumb little kids when I have to teach them how to count and spell and read."

"Would you rather be studying something else?" I asked.

She stared at me for a moment. "What else is there?"

"Nothing here at this college. And teaching is looked down on—anybody can teach, they say."

Her attitude reflected that of many of her classmates, and I set about to change it. I knew teaching little children laid the foundation for all areas of learning, so it had to be important.

How could I get this fact across to my students? Somehow I had to help them realize that the best teachers are needed for the grades.

To stimulate pride in their chosen field, I organized my education students into the first Future Teachers of America Club in Alabama. The FTA is an affiliate of the National Education Association (NEA), which at that time was strictly an educational society. This prestigious national society gave clout to my education students, as well as to all who joined it. With its activities we built up a high self-image for each student, at the same time rendering services to our college. Groups of FTA members sold magazines in nearby cities to raise funds. Others stayed with me, and made sandwiches to sell to hungry schoolmates. We conducted a campus "clean-up" week and took pride in keeping it clean.

Our club activities included a visit to neighboring Alabama State Agricultural and Mechanical Institute at Normal, Alabama, and an overnight trip to Tuskegee Institute. When National Education Week rolled around, we took full charge including worship programs and the Sabbath services. On the concluding Saturday night of the week we provided a cultural program. We did this yearly, often bringing out-of-town artists from New York City, Wisconsin, and Tennessee. Throughout the year we featured outstanding films for a full evening's entertainment. All of these programs were dress-up occasions shared by the entire college and patronized by the community. The FTA paid for all of this from small monthly dues we paid and the money we raised from other projects.

To cap it all off, at the end of the year FTA gave a $100 scholarship to an academy or high school graduate who wished to continue in college at Oakwood and prepare to become a teacher. Nearly all of my own FTA members have at one time been teachers in church schools throughout America. Praise God for the dedicated teachers Oakwood College turned out and for the Christian parents who sacrificed to send their children through church school and on to college.

Growing Pains

Katrina, the smiling girl who had greeted me at the door of the dean's apartment when I first arrived at Oakwood College, had become very close to me. After I had moved from my one-room housing to a small apartment, Katrina was my most frequent visitor. One evening as we sat chatting, she surprised me by saying, "Mama, I wish you would adopt me!"

"Well," I hedged, "you know you are my girl. You're welcome here anytime."

"No," she insisted, "I don't mean that; I mean I want you to legally adopt me. Please, Mama. I am so alone, and you need a daughter too. Someone to care for you when you grow older."

In the end I agreed, and Katrina took care of all the necessary paperwork making her legally mine. She completed her teacher education and took a school down in the Florida Everglades.

Now after some time of teaching in Florida, I called her back to be one of my supervising teachers. She found a little house on campus which had become vacant, and she was determined to get it for us. "Our family is too big for this apartment," she said. "With Chula [my

89

Siamese cat, a replacement for Le Chat, who had been poisoned] and you and me, we need room." I didn't think she could manage it, but soon I found myself being moved into more spacious quarters, much to my delight.

One day several of the young men in my education classes came to see me. "Miss Burrell," the spokesman began, "we would like to see this department expand to offer secondary education." He glanced sideways at his colleagues, who nodded in agreement. One of them picked up the conversation.

"Yes, Miss Burrell," he said, "We feel it's rather demeaning for grown men to be teaching small children. We'd like to be teaching in one of our academies."

That presented a challenge to me, one that seemed rather impossible, yet perhaps it could be done. I promised the young men that I would work on it, and within a few weeks I received permission from the administration to add a few courses in that area. Since I was head of the department, I began begging for another teacher, preferably one trained in secondary education. By the next school year one came, but having been in charge at the post from which he came, it was hard for him to work under someone else. I turned over all the secondary classes to him, and we did learn to work together. The program prospered; we had saved our young men from deserting the field of teaching. Badly as they were needed, it constituted a major victory.

Soon after classes began in the 1951-1952 school year, I began to have trouble with my back and legs. It grew steadily worse, yet I kept up my heavy schedule until one evening the pain was so excruciating I could neither lie down nor sit up, but knelt at my bedside trying to make plans for the next day's classes. Next morning I painfully dragged myself to my first class. I had never excused myself before for lack of preparation, but this morning I had to tell my students, "I'm very sorry, but last night I couldn't prepare the lesson because I had too much pain. But I do know this subject well; so if you have any questions you may ask them, and I'll do my best to answer." The students responded, and we had a most interesting session.

My adopted daughter, Katrina, insisted I get some help, so she notified President Peterson, who suggested I go to our sanitarium in Nashville, Tennessee. He even made arrangements for the college business manager to drive me there.

I arrived at the sanitarium the day before Thanksgiving, and the doctor treated me for arthritis for two weeks. I was no better. He then decided to do a spinal puncture. He suspected cancer of the spine, and this was verified by a myelogram. He told me I could not live very long.

Back at Oakwood the faculty and students decided to hold a three-day fasting and prayer service for my recovery. Even the smallest grade-school child took part. The day after

Christmas I underwent surgery to replace a vertebra and fuse others. The doctors found no sign of cancer. God had answered our prayers. Yet the battle was not over; I still remained very sick, and the prognosis was that I probably would never walk again.

But God and I talked that over. I had made full peace with my Maker and felt resigned to whatever was His will for me. Eventually, I walked. In six months I returned to the classroom and my beloved young people. Like Paul I'll always have "a thorn in the flesh," but I also have evidence of the healing power of God through the prayers of dedicated Christians.

We needed a new elementary school building; I had been begging for one many years, and finally the funds were made available, and the Anna Knight Elementary School became a reality. Most of the specifications my teachers and I requested were granted. I personally raised over $500 for new office furniture.

I am deeply indebted to Oakwood College for keeping me on its payroll during the several summers and two winters when I left campus to study. Thanks, too, to the faithful laboratory school teachers who carried much of my load during my absences. This made it possible for me to earn my B.A. degree from Emmanuel Missionary College (Andrews University) in 1943, my M.S. degree from Wisconsin University in 1948, and my Doctor of Education from Teacher's College, Columbia University in 1959. At last I had reached my goal.

A Working Retirement

The Education Department of the Southern Union had looked favorably upon my work at Oakwood College. Early in 1957 they awarded me the Teacher's Professional Elementary Certificate, the highest certificate given by the General Conference of Seventh-day Adventists. Perhaps this focused the eyes of our Adventist institutions of learning in my direction. That spring I received an invitation to teach a summer graduate course in reading at Potomac University in Washington, D.C.

Oakwood College agreed to loan me to Potomac University for the summer. Later Potomac University moved to the Emmanuel Missionary campus at Berrien Springs, Michigan. I found the change stimulating. Teaching on a graduate level for the first time, I felt challenged by my all-teacher student body. They worked hard, and so did I, but we had fun while learning. I studied, planned, and prayed much. President Dick and Dr. Raymond Moore, dean of the Graduate School, each complimented me because of the good reports that came in from students. I gave the glory to God; He had guided me and given me success.

In the fall I returned to Oakwood College, but the following summer found me working on my doctorate at Columbia University. I resumed my duties at Oakwood in January 1959, having completed all the requirements for my degree, Doctor of Education, which would be awarded in absentia in June 1959.

For over twenty years I had worked with Oakwood's problems and had solved some of them. However, the physical and mental strain had been tremendous. I had made enough "bricks without straw." I was tired, but I voiced no complaint. Through the influence of some of my former schoolmates, now situated in Washington and holding high positions at the General Conference, I decided to resign from Oakwood in May 1961.

A few days later found me in Washington accepting work as a coeditor of the basal reading series. I knew about the denomination's plan to publish new readers to replace the trade books our schools had to use. Such books usually contained some principles contrary to our Seventh-day Adventist beliefs.

Ethel Young, a teacher with broad experience, had been appointed to accomplish the impossible. Since many of our church schools used the readers put out by Scott, Foresman Publishing House, finding them less objectionable than others, the Education Department appealed to Harry House, a Seventh-day Adventist salesman who worked out of Scott, Foresman's main office in Chicago.

We presented our case to Mr. House, and then asked, "Won't you please use your influence to get the company to lend us their expertise and help us develop a series of readers especially for Adventist children?"

He promised to do all he could. After many prayers, letters, telephone calls, and long waiting periods, the answer came.

"Give those Adventists anything they want!" This directive included not only the use of their materials, but also full copyright privileges, access to all the scientific data and expertise of textbook writing, and—as the frosting on the cake—a delightful, first-rate, Christian consultant by the name of Lee Horton!

While waiting for this favor to be granted, Ethel Young had compiled and organized many stories into files. She had a clear-cut idea of how we should proceed, having consulted with Lee Horton at least once before I arrived. Ethel had all kinds of graded word lists and instructions.

Ethel Young, vivacious and enthusiastic, a fully dedicated Christian, threw her whole soul into the work and drew me in with her. I found my desk beside hers; she told me later that when she first moved it in there some of the workers questioned her and seemed surprised that she was so willing to work closely with a black person. But she insisted, "We need to talk together; we'll be working very closely, so I need her right here beside me."

When we walked into the office together that morning, coming up from the general worship service, Ethel cautioned me, "Natelkka, you are on the spot here."

"That doesn't surprise me," I told her. "I'm always on the spot somewhere. Don't let it worry you."

She didn't. I didn't. In a short time no one else did. We rode the elevator together, lunched together, took walks together, and became fast friends, and our work progressed without any ruffled feelings. I still treasure Ethel Young's friendship.

Creating Multi-ethnic Readers

My task as coeditor continued until near the beginning of 1964. During that time Ethel and I zeroed in on the idea of a multi-ethnic reading series. Elder Mathews liked the idea and gave us the go-ahead. If the gospel is to go to all the world, he reasoned, then beginning with their earliest education our Seventh-day Adventist children should absorb an understanding and love for all nationalities and ethnic groups. What better way could they acquaint themselves with each other than through stories of boys and girls like themselves, having the same needs, hopes, and problems, differing only in color and culture?

At that time Scott, Foresman had not produced a multi-ethnic series. However, when we presented the idea to Lee Horton, our consultant, she highly approved it. We could not possibly represent "every nation, and kindred, and tongue and people," yet we did choose one or two typical types from each of our worldwide divisions.

"How shall we begin?" Ethel asked me.

"Right at home?" I suggested. Then a moment later I said, "No, there might be some hurt feelings. How about a displaced European?"

"Excellent!" she responded. Thus the story of Mr. Bell, the displaced European baker, entered the series to the delight of little readers. As the story unfolds, little Sally surprises Mr. Bell with one of Puff's kittens "so he won't be lonesome."

Happy with our success, Ethel and I determined to take a larger step. "Let's take a black child," I suggested, holding my breath.

"Umm. Remember these books will be used in both the North and South," Ethel responded. "Have you any idea how to go about such a story?"

"I think so."

"Good, Natelkka. Then you write it."

I started working on it. The story evolved slowly. White children share their Sabbath School papers with a crippled black boy who cannot run and play. All become good friends. Later stories featuring black children make them the givers, not the recipients. Ethel approved; the book was printed, and children liked the stories.

Encouraged, Ethel and I kept working. We kept the white Dick, Jane, and Sally family, but added a comparable black family with father, mother, a pair of twins, Pam and Penny, and an older brother. There were also grandparents. This called for thousands of dollars in new art, but we all agreed that it was important for white children to be exposed to black children on a comparable level with themselves. We located an artist who did a beautiful job; the pictures of the black children are as fetching as those of the white ones.

Another specific of the Adventist series was that a church unit should be in every book. We made a list of doctrinal points to include; one of our major tasks centered upon writing stories to inculcate these points. We finally narrowed it down to writing stories about the beginning of our different departments—the educational work, the medical work, the Sabbath School, foreign missions, and the young people's work. Sources included the Ellen G. White vault, letters to surviving relatives, interviews, trips to the Smithsonian Institution for American Indian data, and, of course, the libraries. I learned so very much. In trying to help children be proud of Adventism, I became more aware and more appreciative of it myself. Yes, I was very proud to be a Seventh-day Adventist.

My life in Washington did not consist of all work. Although I had to limit my social life because of my physical condition, I found time to visit relatives and friends. Ever since my spinal surgery in 1951 I had suffered with an unpredictable leg; sometimes, in the most embarrassing places, it would just give out on me and I would fall.

But I had several cousins living in Washington and Oakwood students who had married and now lived in the Washington area, all whom I enjoyed visiting.

I did not work steadily during my time in Washington; you might say it was a partial retirement. Appropriations came at intervals according to grade sections—first and second, third and forth, and so forth. I rested in between. Sometimes I did research, but usually I took a trip elsewhere. Each time I returned I had to make new living arrangements; thus I made friends with several families such as The Frank Jacksons, Elder and Mrs. Owen Troy, Sr., and Elder and Mrs. Frank Peterson. All were delightful to live with. During my last term in Washington I rented a small apartment, and bought a car, which solved my transportation problems.

One Friday afternoon as I cleaned my apartment, listening absentmindedly to the music from my TV, it suddenly stopped. A horrible announcement followed:

"President Kennedy has been shot!"

Like most people across our great nation, I stood in the middle of the floor crying "Impossible! Why? Why would anyone do such an awful thing?" A pall hung over all Washington. All offices, including those of our Adventist headquarters, remained closed on Monday, the day of the funeral. Along with thousands of other people, I found myself along the funeral route. Black and white alike waited patiently in a bond of sorrow, as mothers hushed their tired children and solemn soldiers controlled the crowds threatening to overflow into the streets.

Finally we heard the muffled drum beats,

louder as they approached, the drummers beating their slow lament and the varied divisions of Army, Navy, Marines, Coast Guard and Air Force marching in stony silence.

"Look at that beautiful black horse," someone in the crowd whispered loudly.

"See how he's acting up," someone else replied. "The groom can hardly control him." "He's saddled, but riderless!" "A pair of boots in the stirrups. Strange. They're backwards!" That's symbolic, I thought. The horse has lost its rider—our President.

"Neat," approved a teenager standing near me.

"Too bad the horse won't walk quietly," I thought.

"That's Jackie's horse," a viewer explained. "They've got horses trained to walk in a funeral march, but Jackie wanted them to use her horse for the President's last ride."

"Neat," again from the teenager.

Another suggested, "Maybe the horse is rebelling at the senselessness of the President's death."

What a contrast that horse made against the controlled, trimly uniformed American men of all colors as they marched with precision and dignity. Even in my sorrow for the loss of my President, I gloried in America. My own country. Sometimes evil and bad, but also beautiful and good, and the people bonded together there were my own countrymen. In that tragic procession Afro-Americans shared; their blood, sweat and tears had helped make a great country called America. In uniform black men from each defense section looked and performed like all the rest. I took pride in our black men.

The city and the nation continued to mourn until the President's body lay in Arlington Cemetery and the eternal flame blazed above his resting place. Then it reluctantly returned to "business as usual." But that moment in history will never be forgotten by those who lived through it.

By the end of 1963 the series of Adventist church-school readers neared completion. The need for an assistant editor no longer existed; my task was completed. The Education Department presented me with a three-volume set of the *Comprehensive Index to the Writings of Ellen G. White* at the farewell party they gave for me. Sadly, I bade those assembled good-bye; I knew I would miss the camaraderie of those wonderful workers who had accepted me for what I was—a fellow American.

Retirement, Not for Me

After completing the coediting of the readers for the first six grades in our Seventh-day Adventist schools, I made my home with my adopted daughter, Katrina Nesbitt, in Rochester, New York. As a retiree I should have revelled in the fact that I had no more work worries. However, I still lived, and I felt like the man who prayed, "Lord, keep me alive while I'm living." I wanted to be teaching—somebody, something, somewhere.

I decided to volunteer to relieve the Jefferson Avenue teachers, my adopted daughter Katrina, and Margaret Earle, by teaching their language arts classes. They were happy to accept my offer, for it lightened their load; it also gave me access to the children and enlivened my life. The youngsters benefited from the extra attention, their brown eyes rolling at each other as they grinned, "Miss Nesbitt's mother is a big doctor teacher!"

I liked it in Rochester. I even considered applying for part-time teaching at Rochester University; the pay was tempting, my qualifications adequate. But deep in my heart my teenage resolution reminded me, "Remember. Be a teacher for Jesus." Could I be that kind of teacher at the University of Rochester? Perhaps. One could serve God anywhere, but never did my heart answer Yes. I bided my time.

The winter passed, and with spring came an invitation to teach during the twelve-week summer session at Andrews University. Again I accepted without mentioning terms; it had to be right; I'd be doing God's work. The university had reserved one of its well-furnished apartments in the Garland Apartment complex for me. An office had been set up for me in Nethery Hall. What memories that evoked.

During my last summer as a student on this campus Nethery Hall boasted the title of "New Administration Building." It was 1943. Now, the summer of 1964, here I was occupying one of its offices as a teacher. Did God have this in mind for me all those years?

I recalled an incident of that '43 summer. I had just finished vacuuming the living room in Birch Hall, the women's dormitory, and had returned the vacuum to the custodian's office in the basement of the building. As I passed Nethery Hall on my way to my room, the dean of men came out the front door and fell into step beside me.

After the usual greeting, he said, "You'll be teaching here next year, won't you." It was more of a statement than a question.

Astonished, I answered, "Not to my knowledge."

"Well, you ought to be," he stated, and hurried on.

What could have gone on in that faculty meeting the dean had just attended, I wondered. Me! A teacher at Andrews University? As much prejudice as existed on campus at that time— separate tables in the dining room, white students refusing to say "Good morning" or "Excuse me" to black ones, an administration that seemed to condone such bigotry! Ask me to teach here? That, I decided, must certainly be the impossible dream.

Yet here I was in 1964, settling in as an honored teacher. If any such prejudice still existed at what was now Andrews University, none of my colleagues or students ever showed it to me or to any of the black students who dotted the campus. Times had really changed. God had been at work; brotherly love enfolded the university campus in one big fellowship of Christianity.

Two fellow teachers, Dr. Merlene Ogden and Dr. Richard Schwartz, held offices in proximity to mine. On numerous occasions each of them answered my questions and acted as guides acquainting me with the intricacies surrounding work in a large establishment of learning. I held classes in Nethery Hall too, one of them in the same room where once I had been a student. The same uneven board remained in the floor (replaced later when the room was carpeted). I prayed as I taught there that I might be the inspiration to my students that my professor,

Dr. H. M. Tippett, had been to me.

At the end of the summer, as I prepared to return to Rochester, the chairman of the department protested, "But Miss Burrell, we expect you to remain in the department."

"Oh?" I answered. "I understood I had been hired for the summer only."

"No, indeed. We want you to stay indefinitely."

Thus I became a permanent "guest professor" at Andrews Unversity. During my teaching at Andrews University in the 1969-71 school years I also worked on the seventh and eighth-grade readers for the denomination, thus completing the series.

My first three winters at Andrews would have been extremely difficult had it not been for Elder Robert Douglas and his wife, Madge, friends from Oakwood College days. They lived in the village of Berrien Springs while Elder Douglas attended graduate classes in the seminary. The long walk from my apartment to my office would have taxed my back and legs to the limit, but Elder Douglas came for me each morning and drove me to my office in time for my 7:30 classes. In due time, I bought my own car, but Elder Douglas's kindness will always be remembered.

Since I had been involved with the Adventist reading series, it seemed fitting that I teach methods in reading. And because I had a heavy concentration in psychology in my graduate program, I also taught a class in that subject each quarter. To keep up with new developments in each field, I read and studied assiduously in order to give my students the newest ideas, tempered with my own experiences and fitted into the framework of the Master Teacher.

In retrospect, I feel I came nearest to meeting the needs of my students in the psychology courses. This discipline presents many wonderful opportunities to direct minds to the Creator, giving an understanding of human needs and God's way of supplying them. I tried to make all my teaching Christ-centered; to a degree, I think I succeeded. I greatly enjoyed my teaching days at Andrews University.

During breaks between summer and fall classes Katrina and I usually vacationed somewhere—going to New Brunswick, Canada, or to her campus "sisters" Julie, Mildred, and Katie in Pennsylvania and Washington, D.C., or to my close friends, the W. D. Smiths in the Bronx.

At the end of the spring session at Andrews in 1965 I went to Rochester to be with Katrina while she underwent surgery, returning to Andrews in time for the summer session. A week later Katrina herself drove out in time to attend a class. When summer school finished, we took a trip to Niagara Falls and enjoyed a real rest before resuming our teaching loads for the year.

Through the years many changes came to Andrews. My office gave way to other departments and was moved several times, but always in the back of the minds of those in the Education Department was the question, "When can we have our own building?" Just east of Nethery Hall stood a building labeled "Education." It had been earmarked for us, but in the meantime, it held the elementary school and academy. But the Education Department, which was struggling for recognition, could not attain its goal until we had a building of our own. Solution? Build two new schools! One became the Ruth E. Murdoch Elementary School, and the other housed the academy. Gradually, we moved into our remodeled building and received our proper accreditation. But not before I had shared an office for some time with Dr. Ruth Murdoch, at her kind invitation. We got along famously and became fast friends.

What did all this have to do with me? Everything. I lived through these changes, I became a part of them; I helped in the discussion about them and did my teaching in their aura. I felt happy to be a participant in the healing of the growing pains of my alma mater.

A New Family—A New Home

In the fall of 1967 the quietness of my little apartment succumbed to the noise of teenagers. During the summer, as I rested in Katrina's home in Rochester, I learned that one of her eighth grade graduates, Irene, would not be able to attend church school but must attend a public school for the first time in her eight years of schooling. Irene frequently visited us; usually she made some reference to her unhappy prospect for the next school year. I talked it over with Katrina; then I offered, "Irene, how would you like to come live with me and attend Andrews Academy?"

Her response was spontaneous. Throwing her arms around me, she cried, "Do you mean it? Really?" Assuring her that I did, we obtained permission for her to come. Irene had a deep interest in music and decided while in academy to major in it. I went with her to register, and we made an appointment for a voice test. When the time came, I directed her to the music building. I expected her to return within an hour or two at the most. But two hours passed, and still no

Irene. Four hours later she appeared.

"Where on earth have you been?" I asked her.

"Oh, I met a boy, and he offered to show me around the campus," she replied.

It was time for me to set limits. I did. But the young man persisted. I told Irene to bring him home with her, and I explained to both of them why he could not monopolize her time; she was too young for courtship. She had come for an education. I had no objection to friendship in a group, but no twosomes. They took my advice, and the boy sometimes came with other friends to our house, but we had no trouble keeping Irene's priorities straight. Understandably, she had been flattered by his attention; it was her first time away from home, and to be singled out among so many gave her confidence among her group of friends.

I took Irene to meet the Roger Smith family. Their daughters, Meredith and Margie, took her in as though she were a new sister. Their brother, Sonny, made a good substitute for Irene's brothers at home. Soon Irene filled our house with her friends. Brenda Valentine, a day student who commuted, often spent Friday nights with her, and their bedtime giggles were hard to control, but eventually they slept.

I found bringing up a teenager to be a new experience, yet a challenging one, often fun but sometimes frustrating. But between my teaching, which I loved, and the constant association of teenagers in the home I had no time to grow old. My seventy-second birthday found me fulfilled and happy. Yet Katrina worried about my living so independently. She, better than others, knew how fragile my physical condition had become; I could not hide from her, as I did from others, my increasing discomfort.

After twenty-five years as a church-school teacher, successful in her own right, she decided to "retire" and make a home for me. She came to Andrews in time for the 1968 summer session, and we looked for a permanent home. We found a nice duplex close to the university. Katrina moved her furniture from Rochester, and since some of mine was still stored at Oakwood, it meant a double move.

But eventually we were settled in our comfortable home, and we decided to visit Katie and Mildred in Pennsylvania. While visiting we became alerted to another problem which would again change the family structure of our home.

The Family Grows

Carla, Mildred's daughter, had graduated that summer from Pine Forge Academy. She wanted very much to go on to college, as her older brother, Michael, was doing. But Mildred saw no way to finance two children in college, yet she prayed that Carla might have a chance too.

Could we squeeze Carla into the room with Irene, Katrina and I asked each other? Yes, we could, and so the offer was made—free room and board; Mildred would only have to pay tuition. Carla could work some to help with that.

I now had a real family—a daughter, Katrina; a "grandchild," Carla; and Irene, who with a mother and a foster-mother of her own, remained a little hesitant about calling me "mother" yet considered herself my child. For me, the situation presented a minor replica of my days as dean at Oakwood—conducting family worship, getting everyone up on time, overseeing breakfast and a reasonable amount of room care before everyone rushed off to classes. Then keeping track of schedules, supervising study periods, making time for individual mother-daughter chats and answering the normal questions arising from growth and new experiences.

There were no dull moments during the years Carla and Irene lived with us. Occasional pouts and tears when wills clashed, but these were compensated for many occasions of bubbling laughter, music and song.

Katrina and I decided to give Irene a gala party on her sixteenth birthday. Carla acted as hostess; the house bulged with Irene's friends, both male and female, all bearing gifts. Sixteen candles adorned the birthday cake Katrina decorated. A large bowl of punch, repeatedly filled, complimented the delicious salad supper. My own happiness in providing this treat for Irene helped me understand my own mother's pleasure in the parties she gave for me through the years. And between lulls in filling the punch bowl I reminisced.

I remembered my eighth or ninth birthday. Because Bonnie, my maternal grandmother, lay terminally ill in one bedroom, Mother had worked hard to meet expenses for doctors and medicines, and there was no money for parties. However, Mother didn't let my birthday pass unnoticed. She invited two little girls, sisters, to come spend the afternoon with me. We played quietly in my room with toys and dolls, mindful of my ailing grandmother, until Mother suggested a taffy pull. She helped us get started, and then the doctor appeared.

"Where is Natelkka?" he asked, as he always

did. Finding me in the kitchen, he asked, "What are you girls doing?" He watched as we stretched the whitening taffy into interesting shapes.

"Pulling taffy," I told him. "It's my birthday."

"Your birthday!" he exclaimed. "And no ice cream!" He reached in his pocket and pulled out a dollar bill. "Here, Natelkka. Take this and buy some ice cream for your friends and yourself."

I looked questioningly at Mother. She nodded her approval, so I thanked him profusely. Then as Mother had directed us, we girls ran across the street and bought a quart of vanilla ice cream and another quart of strawberry ice cream. Frankly, I cannot remember which tasted better, the taffy or the ice cream. The taffy lasted longer, but the memory is forever.

My sixteenth summer brought another party. Since my February birthday had passed while I was at boarding school, Mother gave me a party that summer. The young people from the church were my guests. Mother watched us play various games as she went back and forth from the living room to the kitchen. The game we enjoyed the most was called "Wink-um." The boys stood behind chairs, the girls sat in them, but one chair was empty. The boy who succeeded in "winking" a girl to his empty chair was expected to "kiss" her. These were far from movie and TV versions of kisses; they involved at most a peck on the cheek or forehead or top of the head.

One of the young men at the party was a visitor from Dutch Guiana, now known as Surinam, a recent convert to Adventism, eager to return to his country with an American wife to help him evangelize his people. Without my consent he had decided I was the girl. I disliked him heartily. Whenever in the game his chair became empty, I refused to look in his direction, so he never had a chance to "kiss" me.

The following Sabbath, Elder Humphrey, our pastor, called all of the girls who had attended my party into his office. He lectured us on how sinful we had been, and looking straight at me, he said, "And you, Natelkka. I am surprised that you would let a boy pollute your lips!"

None of us said a word; we just looked solemn. But I wondered what Elder Humphrey could mean; no one had "polluted" my lips or anyone else's at my party. Mother had watched it all; she knew the "kisses" had more often landed on an ear or a topknot than anywhere near our lips. I didn't feel I had done anything wrong.

Later, I learned that Mrs. Humphrey had asked the boy from Dutch Guiana how he liked the party. He replied, "Oh, I had a good time at the party. I got to kiss the American girls, all except Natelkka. She wouldn't let me kiss her!" I laughed at the memory.

At Andrews my family continued to grow. Irene's brother, Gerrard Brathwaite (Jerry to us) came to college, and although he lived in the dormitory, he counted our home as his. Katrina had been his teacher; I had taught both Jerry and his brother, as well as Irene in grade school.

A year later Collins, another brother, transferred from Oakwood to attend the seminary at Andrews. Both boys came often, sometimes alone, but often with roommates or friends— sometimes special friends of the opposite sex.

Now they have all gone, except Jerry. Collins has a pastorate in Virginia; Irene completed the nurse's course and married. She has two children, Levi III, named after her husband Levi Woodward, and Melanie. Carla graduated from Andrews with a psychology major; she now works in Kalamazoo while continuing her studies for a master's degree. And dear Jerry, what would I do without him?

Through the years he has been my "right-hand man." While working his entire way through college, working nights and attending a few classes during the day, he has found time to take me to my various appointments. I gave up driving several years ago. Jerry is our man about the house; he does minor repairs and yard work. He is truly a son, and I love him. His name for me is Mother.

I fully believe God gave me Katrina as a daughter. Ours is a beautiful mother-daughter relationship. She means everything to me; she could do no more for me if she were my born-in-the-flesh daughter. Her every thought seems to be for my comfort. When she gave up church-school teaching to come and care for me, she had no prospects of a job. But she soon found one in the Benton Harbor school district, a city about twelve miles from Berrien Springs. She has taught at Bard School now for thirteen years. In a competition with over 500 teachers in the system she was acclaimed Teacher of the Year for 1978.

I am proud of my daughter, Katrina. She is, of course, a product of Oakwood College, from which she graduated years ago and from which she received initial training. Actually, I'm proud of all my Oakwood daughters. Mildred became a successful teacher and spent many years as a church-school teacher, as well as some years teaching in public school. Julie works in public school as a counselor. Katie is a statistical secretary for the Allegheny East Conference. And while each went on to continue her growth, they received their foundation at Oakwood College. And it is there that we became a "family."

Kaleidoscopic Happenings

My continuing years at Andrews University run through my mind like pieces of colored glass in a kaleidoscope. So many rich experiences and valued associations! Interesting students, troubled students, the wonderful opportunity to meet and often teach people of various nationalities and cultures. What joy to become acquainted with them as real flesh-and-blood people, not merely nonentities in a geography or history book or some unsaved somebody for whom we give a Thirteenth Sabbath Offering to keep. Simply lovable, delightful people from everywhere.

I shake the kaleidoscope and watch the varied colors come into view—students who have poured out their hearts to me and with whom I have knelt in prayer. See that ruby-colored piece? That's the late-night call from Chicago. "I'm just calling to say good-bye. I'm going to kill myself; I'm half drunk, and I have a bottle of pills handy. Remember, I'm a nurse, and I know how to do it. You were good to me—just wanted you to know." Then bang went the receiver, before I could shout, "Where are you? Wait!" I couldn't lose that student now; she trusted me; she was crying out for help. I alerted the police and prayed. Oh, how I prayed! The young lady still comes to visit me.

Ah! That dark blue piece—a fine, industrious Christian young man. He's worked hard, long hours, yet at registration time he hasn't saved enough for a new term. His friends are going on; he's discouraged, even tempted to give up. God doesn't seem to answer his prayers for help. "How much do you need to take the course you'll need this term?" I ask. He tells me, and I write out a check for the amount.

At the end of the term the young man comes to me. "Thanks, Mother," he says. "That Bible course I took this term really saved me; I was on my way out when you gave me that check."

Do you see those little pieces of yellow? They represent the home-cooked dinners for various cafeteria-fed students. Did you ever hear of young people clamoring to wash dishes? These did. "It makes us feel like we're at home," was their reason.

There's a piece like royal purple of the East. It must be the young East Indian mother of two fine boys who lived in Garland Apartments. She came to my apartment often for help in dealing with the older boy's jealousy of his brother. How the light flashes as she tells me, "My boys are fine now. You helped so much." I never meant to be a counselor, just a good teacher. I never could separate the two.

The kaleidoscope scintillates with numerous pieces representing classroom incidents. For many students I was their first experience with an Afro-American teacher. All were courteous, but often I sensed an expectancy. "What's she like?" This didn't bother me; I ignored it completely. To me, each student came as God's beloved and chosen child, one He had entrusted to me briefly to teach. Their response was beautiful.

As time passed, students requested to be allowed to take my classes. Sometimes I'd meet an unknown student on campus, and he would say, "Oh, I've heard about you. I hope to take one of your classes." Or again, "I'm so disappointed that I haven't been able to work in one of your classes, Dr. Burrell." I ceased being an oddity.

But the education faculty and secretaries still marveled. Twice retired, at the age of 69 I had begun a new career at Andrews University. On my seventieth birthday they greeted me with admiration; on my seventy-second they honored me with an office party, saying "You show no sign of aging." When I turned seventy-five, Dr. Akers, professor of religious education, hosted an evening worship period in my honor, surprising me with eulogies by former Oakwood students and followed by a salad supper and a huge candle-lighted cake. And on each of my birthdays students also remembered me with small gifts—a plant, a card, sometimes cake and punch.

When my eightieth birthday arrived and I was

still teaching, the staff went to a great deal of planning and work for a program. The big surprise consisted of an immense cake ordered by my former dean, Miss Rachel Christman, who had retired and moved to another state.

The brilliance of the kaleidoscopic colors representing the education faculty cannot be excelled. My immediate colleagues were wonderful. We worked, planned, played, laughed, and prayed together. We still have a healthy concern for each other. I wish it were possible to write a paragraph about each of these fine Christian workers, but space forbids.

How can I fail to mention the small, glittering silvery pieces of the kaleidoscope! They represent the many secretaries and readers who have taken my messages, cared for my mail, checked records, run errands for me, or rushed materials that I needed for my classes. Their nimble fingers and willing hearts added much to the success of my teaching career.

Do you see that black piece? That stands for my tears and the tears of a student I had to fail in a course. Have you ever seen a grown man cry? He came from South America; studying in English was very difficult for him. He often misunderstood and never passed tests unless I coached him on the questions he had missed and then retested him. Even then a "C" was the best grade he could earn. I knew failure meant disgrace at home, yet what could I do? I tried over and over to pull him through, but in good conscience I could not do it—so our tears.

That light blue piece that keeps reappearing. It's one of the secretaries. She had constant problems at home with her teenagers. When she shared her problems with me, we prayed together about them. My understanding and suggestions gave her comfort and strength; her need kept me close to our Saviour. Those children are doing well now, thanks to answered prayer.

As I shake the kaleidoscope, I keep seeing three large pieces of bright red. They are the chairpersons of the department under whom I have been fortunate enough to work. The first is Dr. Chase; I hardly knew him before he left for California and the second took his place—Dr. George Akers. When Dr. Akers was called to the presidency of Columbia Union College, he was replaced by Dr. T. S. Geraty, and I worked under him until my retirement in 1977.

Here I find a multi-colored piece. It must be Dr. Mercedes Dyer—teacher, counselor, chairperson now of the Department of Education, and my close neighbor and friend. How I wish I could tell you of all the other pieces which represent good friends, colleagues, workers, and students. Perhaps at another time and another place.

My activities were not confined to the campus. I often lectured to teachers and students, both in the elementary schools and the high school in Benton Harbor, and on several occasions I was invited to represent my church on Women's Day or Education Day in other churches. Troubled students or parents still come to my home for advice and prayer. Two former students, now teachers in nearby towns, have invited me to give the graduation address for their eighth graders.

A few bright pieces now come into view on the kaleidoscope to remind me of the weddings of my Andrews University acquired children, Lynne, Irene, and Brenda. What exciting times! Those tiny pieces jumping in and out are their children—Lynne and Fleance's young son, Irene and Levi's just-beginning-school son and little sister, Melanie.

Another good shake reveals three dazzling pieces, Ruth, Esther, and Naomi Cooper, whose parents took me in before they were born. Although their mother passed away early and their father passed away in the summer of 1980, they have always kept in touch with me and continue to provide tender, loving concern for their "Big Sister." Floating into view is a piece for "Baby" Harold Cooper, now a grown man—a staff photographer for a prestigious New York company. He, with Ruth's son, Darnley Small (Buddy), provide transportation and an extra measure of love for me when I go home to the Big City.

Then there are some gray pieces I've tried to avoid. They represent loved ones now asleep—a long, slender piece standing for Walter D. Smith, my play "brother," reading companion, and friend of many years. One is for my country-cousin teacher, Fannie, who kept me in touch with my Virginia relatives. That pearl-gray one is Emmelly V. Parris, Walter's sister-in-law, his wife's twin sister. Now Martha Smith lives alone, cared for by Walter's sons, who love her dearly. And of course that newest one is for Dad Cooper, whom I have already mentioned.

A large yellow piece shows up at every turn of the kaleidoscope because it represents my mother's prayers for her tiny neonate. Like the son in Christ's parable who said No! to his father's request then later did his bidding, so this rebel, Natelkka Burrell, returned to our Lord's vineyard and worked many years with a contrite heart. All along the way, God encouraged me with little signs of His approval.

Although my physical body gradually weakened, my mind has remained clear and active. After I resigned at the close of the spring session in 1977, I have been called back from time to time to teach a special course or to address the students in training.

The hidden pieces of my kaleidoscope, when given a vigorous shake, reveal a series of honors accorded to me down through the years.

1945: A Teacher's Life Certificate, presented by the Southern Union for the General Conference.

1958: A Professional Elementary Certificate, the General Conference's highest.

1963: A beautiful corsage and a plaque honoring me as an "author, educator and friend" presented by the Education Department of Andrews University.

1964: A large plaque from the Chicago Chapter of the Oakwood College Alumni Association, bearing the words, "A living inspiration to education."

1972: A citation of honor from the Education Department of the General Conference.

1972: A testimonial dinner at Wynn Schuler's given by the Michiana Chapter of the Oakwood College Alumni. They presented me with two dozen yellow tea roses and a gold watch, plus a plaque with the inscription "for aiding and abetting Christian education above and beyond the call of duty."

1973: Elected to Andrews University's "Hall of Fame," the university's highest honor.

1975: A large plaque presented by the faculty and students of Oakwood College in recognition of "your distinguished contributions to Christian education during more than forty years of dedicated service in teaching, administration, research, and writing."

1975: A citation by the General Conference at its world conference in Vienna, Austria, as one of the ten most outstanding women in the Seventh-day Adventist Church.

1978: The high honor of delivering the commencement address at the spring graduation of my alma mater, Andrews University.

All glory to God, who has been able to take this weak, defective, rebellious bit of humanity and use it so effectively to accomplish His purposes!